Selected Poems

Selected Poems
by
Walt Whitman

Edited by
Lisa Lipkin

CASTLE BOOKS

This edition published in 2000 by
CASTLE BOOKS
A division of Book Sales, Inc.
114 Northfield Avenue
Edison, NJ 08837

ISBN 0-7858-1283-0

PRINTED IN THE UNITED STATES OF AMERICA

Table of Contents

CALAMUS 73

CHILDREN OF ADAM   77

DRUM-TAPS   101

MEMORIES OF PRESIDENT LINCOLN   123

NATURE, MAN AND SELF   135

Preface

✤

When a small volume of poems called *Leaves of Grass* landed on the desks of a handful of New York literary editors in 1855, no one quite knew what to make of it.

"Who is this arrogant young man who proclaims himself the Poet of the Time, and who roots like a pig among a rotten garbage of licentious thoughts?" asked a critic for the New York Daily Times. In fact, the "arrogant young man" was Walt Whitman, and although few could see it at the time, his bold, sensuous, verse would not only revolutionize poetry, but would give birth to a distinctly American voice.

Whitman started *Leaves of Grass*, a small collection of twelve poems, in 1848, but it was so unusual in its form and content that no one would agree to publish it. Seven years later, he published the work himself, stating in the introduction, "The United States themselves are essentially the greatest poem." That first edition received accolades from Ralph Waldo Emerson, who allowed Whitman to reprint his congratulatory letter in the second edition in 1856. All told, there would be six editions of *Leaves of Grass*, affording Whitman the opportunity to continuously sharpen and perfect the work that he believed "had grown with his own emotional and intellectual development."

Whitman was, above all, a New Yorker; born in Long Island in 1819, and raised in Brooklyn. Many of his poems reveal his ongoing love affair with the city. At age 12, Whitman, who was one of nine siblings, went to work as a printer, thereby acquainting himself with great writers like Shakespeare and Homer, who would inspire his passion for words.

In 1836, when Whitman was just 17, he begrudgingly began a teaching career in a one-room schoolhouse in Long Island—a vocation he would often complain about—although it wasn't until 1841 that he left education to become a full-time journalist for a variety of New York newspapers. In addition to a brief stint as an editor in New Orleans, he also tried his hand at fiction, writing several novels; but it was in poetry that Whitman was able to find his most unique and powerful voice.

During the Civil War, Whitman traveled to Washington, D.C. to visit his brother who was recovering from a war injury, and decided to stay and volunteer in the area's military hospitals. Although earning only a modest living as a government clerk, he regularly donated money and supplies for patients who were still recovering from the brutal war. After suffering a stroke in 1873, Whitman moved to Camden, NJ, where he spent his remaining years writing poetry and articles.

A line in a review by Lloyd's Weekly London Newspaper in 1868 serves as the perfect tribute to this remarkable man: "Let people quarrel as they please about what is or is not poetry; but Mr. Walt Whitman is beyond all question a poet."

Introduction

✤

As originally published in
The Atlantic Monthly, February 1902

REMINISCENCES OF WALT WHITMAN
By John Townsend Trowbridge

I first made acquaintance with Whitman's writings when a newspaper notice of the earliest edition of *Leaves of Grass* reached me, in Paris, in the autumn of 1855. It was the most exhilarating piece of news I had received from America during the six months of my absence abroad. Such vigor, such graphic force, such human sympathy, such scope and audacity in the choice and treatment of themes, found in me an eagerly interested reader of the copious extracts which the notice contained. When I came to see the volume itself—the thin, small quarto of 1855—I found in it much that impressed me as formless and needlessly offensive; and these faults were carried to extremes in the second and enlarged edition of 1856. Yet the tremendous original power of this new bard, and the freshness, as of nature itself, which breathed though the best of his songs or sayings, continued to hold their spell over me, and inspired me with intense curiosity as to the man himself. But I had no opportunity of meeting him till he came to Boston in the spring of 1860, to put his third edition through the press.

Then, one day, I was stopped on Washington Street by a friend who made this startling announcement: "Walt Whitman is in town; I have seen him!" When I asked where, he replied: "At the stereotype foundry, just around the corner. Come along! I'll take you to him." The author of *Leaves of Grass* had loomed so large in my imagination as to seem almost super-human; and I was filled with some such feeling of wonder and astonishment as if I had been invited to meet Socrates or King Solomon.

We found a large, gray-haired and gray-bearded, plainly dressed man, reading proof-sheets at a desk in a little dingy office, with a lank, unwholesome-looking lad at his elbow, listlessly watching him. The man was Whitman, and the proofs were those of his new edition. There was a scarcity of chairs, and Whitman, rising to receive us, offered me his; but we all remained standing except the sickly looking lad, who kept his seat until Whitman turned to him and said, "You'd better go now; I'll see you this evening." After he had gone out, Whitman explained: "He is a friend-less boy I found at my boarding place. I am trying to cheer him up and strengthen him with my magnetism." My readers may think this a practi-cal but curiously prosaic illustration of these powerful lines in the early poems:

> "To any one dying, thither I speed and twist the knob of the
>   door.
> I seize the descending man, I raise him with resistless will.
> Every room of the house do I fill with an armed force, lovers of
>   me, bafflers of graves."

The difference between the prosaic fact and the poetic expression was not greater than the contrast between Whitman as I had imagined him and the simple, well-mannered man who stood and talked to us. From his own descriptions of himself, and from the swing and impetus of his lines, I had pictured him proud, alert, grandiose, defiant of the usages of soci-ety; and I found him the quietest of men. I really remember but one thing he said, after sending away the boy. The talk turning on his proof-sheets, I asked how the first poems impressed him, at this re-reading; to which he replied, "I am astonished to find myself capable of feeling so much. " The conversation was all very quiet, pitched in a low key, and I went away somewhat disappointed that he did not say or do something extraordinary and admirable; one of the noticeable things about him being an absence of all effort to make a good impression.

I got on vastly better with him when, the next Sunday morning, he came out to see me on Prospect Hill, in Somerville, where I was then liv-ing. The weather was perfect—it was early May; the few friends I introduced to him were congenial spirits; he was happy and animated, and we spent the day together in such hearty and familiar intercourse that when I parted with him in the evening, on East Cambridge bridge, having walked with him thus far on his way back to Boston, I felt that a large, new friendship had shed a glow on my life. Of much of that day's talk I have a vivid recollection—even of its trivialities. He was not a loud laugher, and rarely made a joke, but he greatly enjoyed the pleasantries of others. He liked especially any allusion, serious or jocular, to his poems. When, at dinner, preparing my dish of salad, I remarked that I was employed as his critics would be when his new editions was out, he queried, "Devouring *Leaves of Grass*?" "No," I said, "cutting up *Leaves of Grass*"—which amused him more, I fancy, than the cutting up did which came later. As the afternoon waned, and he spoke of leaving us, somebody placed a book before the face of the clock. I said "Put *Leaves of Grass* there. Nobody can see through that." "Not even the author?" he said, with a whimsical lifting of the brows.

Much of the talk was about himself and his poems, in every particular of which I was profoundly interested. He told me of his boyhood in Brooklyn; going to work in a printing office at the age of fourteen; teaching school at seventeen and eighteen; writing stories and sketches for periodicals under his full name, Walter Whitman, after which he discarded "Walter" for "Walt"); editing newspapers and making political speeches, on the Democratic side; leading an impulsive, irregular sort of life, and absorbing, as probably no other man ever did the common aspects of the cities he was so proud of, Brooklyn and New York. His friendships were mostly with the common people—pilots, drivers, mechanics; and his favorite diversions, crossing the ferries, riding on the top of omnibuses, and attending operas. He liked to get off alone by the seashore, read Homer and Ossian with the salt air on his cheeks, and shout their winged words to the winds and waves. The book he knew best was the Bible, the prophetical parts of which stirred in him a vague desire to be the bard or prophet of his own time and country.

Then, at the right moment, he read Emerson.

I was extremely interested to know how far the influence of our greatest writer had been felt in the making of a book which, without being at all imitative, was pitched in the very highest key of self-reliance. In his letter to Emerson, printed in the second edition of *Leaves of Grass*, speaking of "Individuality, that new moral American continent," Whitman had averred: "Those shores you found; I say, you led the States there—have led me there." And it seemed hardly possible that the first determined attempt to cast into literature a complete man, with all his pride and passions, should have been made by one whose feet were not already firmly planted on "those shores." Then there was the significant fact of his having mailed a copy of his first edition to Emerson.

Whitman talked frankly on the subject, that day on Prospect Hill, and told how he became acquainted with Emerson's writings. He was at work as a carpenter (his father's trade before him) in Brooklyn, building with his own hands and on his own account small and very plain houses for laboring men; as soon as one was finished and sold, beginning another—houses of two or three rooms. This was in 1854; he was then thirty-five years old. He lived at home with his mother; going of to his work in the morning and returning at night, carrying his dinner pail like any common laborer. Along with his pail he usually carried a book, between which and his solitary meal he would divide his nooning. Once the book chanced to be a volume of Emerson; and from that time he took with him no other writer. His half-formed purpose, his vague aspirations, all that had lain smouldering so long within him, waiting to be fired, rushed into flame at the touch of those electric words—the words that burn in the prose-poem "Nature," and in the essays on "Spiritual Laws," "The Over-Soul," and "Self-Reliance." The sturdy carpenter in his working-day garb, seated on his pile of boards; a poet in that rude disguise, as yet but dimly conscious of his powers; in one hand the sandwich put up for him by his good mother, his other hand holding open the volume that revealed to him his greatness and his destiny—this is the picture which his simple narrative called up, that Sunday so long ago, and which has never faded from my memory.

He freely admitted that he could never have written his poems if he had not first "come to himself," and that Emerson helped him to "find himself." I asked if he thought he would have come to himself without that help. He said, "Yes, but it would have taken longer." And he used this characteristic expression: "I was simmering, simmering, simmering; Emerson brought me to a boil."

It was in that summer of 1854, while he was still at work upon his houses, that he began the *Leaves of Grass*, which he wrote, rewrote, and re-rewrote (to quote again his own words), and afterward set in type with his own hand.

I make this statement thus explicit because a question of profound personal and literary interest is involved, and because it is claimed by some of the later friends of Whitman that he wrote his first *Leaves of Grass* before he had read Emerson. When they urge his own authority for their contention, I can only reply that he told me distinctly the contrary, when his memory was fresher.

The Emersonian influence is often clearly traceable in Whitman's early poems; seldom in the later. It is in the first line of the very first poem in which he struck the keynote of his defiant chant: "I celebrate myself." Yet the form Whitman chose for his message was as independent of Emerson's as of all other literary forms whatsoever. Outwardly, his unrhymed and unmeasured lines resemble those of Tupper's Proverbial Philosophy; but in no other way are they akin to those colorless platitudes. To the music of the opera, for which he had a passion, more than to anything else, was due his emancipation from what he called the "ballad style" of poetry, by which he meant poetry hampered by rhyme and metre. "But for the opera," he declared, that day on Prospect Hill, "I could never have written *Leaves of Grass*."

Whitman was at that time a man of striking personal appearance, as indeed he always was: fully six feet tall, and large proportionally; slow of movement, and inclined to walk with a lounging gait, which somebody has likened to an "elephantine roll." He wore his shirt collar open at the throat, exposing his hairy chest, in decidedly unconventional fashion. His necktie was drawn into a loose knot, or hung free, with serpentine ends coiled away somewhere in his clothing. He was scrupulously neat in person—"never dressed in black, always dressed freely and clean in strong clothes," according to his own description of himself; head massive, complexion florid-tawny, forehead seamed with wrinkles, which, along with his premature grayness, made him look much older than he was. Mr. Howells, in his First Impressions of Literary New York, describes a meeting with him a few months later, that same year (1860), and calls him "the benign old man." Whitman was at that time forty-one.

I did not see him again for three years and a half: meanwhile the Civil War was raging, and in 1862 he went to the front, to nurse his brother, Lieutenant Colonel George W. Whitman, who had been wounded at Fredericksburg. This was the beginning of his hospital work, which became so important an episode in his life.

In the latter part of November, 1863, a fortunate circumstance placed me in friendly relations with Salmon P. Chase, then at the summit of his fame as Secretary of the Treasury in Lincoln's Cabinet, and I became a guest in his house.

I had at that time few acquaintances in Washington. One of the most prized of these was William Douglas O'Connor. He had turned aside from literature, in which we who knew him in the flower of his youthful promise had believed him destined to excel, and entered a department of the government—one of those vast mausoleums in which so many talents, small and great, have been buried, and brave ambitions have turned quietly to dust. His first employment was in the Treasury; in the Treasury, also, when I first knew him, was that other valiant friend of Whitman's, John Burroughs, who, fortunately for himself and his readers, escaped O'Connor's fate. When O'Connor left the Treasury it was to enter the Lighthouse Board, where he became head clerk, and sat like a spider in the midst of his web, a coast light at the end of each invisible line, hundreds of thousands of miles away. In those useful radiations the beams of his genius became too deeply immersed to shine otherwise than fitfully in what I always deemed his proper sphere.

I knew of his intimacy with Whitman, and when one day I found him at his office, and had answered his many questions, telling him where I was domiciled, one of the first I asked in return was, "Where's Walt?"— the familiar name by which Whitman was known to his friends.

"What a chance!" said O'Connor, in his ardent way. "Walt is here in Washington, living close by you, within a stone's throw of the Secretary's door. Come to my house on Sunday evening, and I will have him there to meet you."

On seeing him again at O'Connor's, I found Whitman but little changed, except that he was more trimly attired, wearing a loosely fitting but quite elegant suit of black—yes, black at last! He was in the best of spirits; and I remember with what a superb and joyous pace he swung along the street, between O'Connor and me, as we walked home with him, after ten o'clock.

Diagonally opposite to Chase's great house, on the corner of E and 6th streets, stood one of those old wooden buildings which then and for some years afterwards lingered among the new and handsome blocks rising around them, and made the "city of magnificent distances" also a city of astonishing architectural contrasts. In the fine, large mansion, sumptuously furnished, cared for by sleek and silent colored servants, and thronged by distinguished guests, dwelt the great statesman; in the old tenement opposite, in a bare and desolate back room, up three flights of stairs, quite alone, lived the poet. Walt led the way up those dreary stairs, partly in darkness, found the keyhole of a door which he unlocked and opened, scratched a match, and welcomed us to his garret.

Garret it literally was, containing hardly any more furniture than a bed, a cheap pine table, and a little sheet-iron stove in which there was no fire. A window was open, and it was a December night. But Walt, clearing a chair or two of their litter of newspapers, invited us to sit down and stop awhile, with as simple and sweet hospitality as if he had been offering us the luxuries of the great mansion across the square.

Sit down we did (O'Connor on the bed, as I remember), and "drank delight of battle" over books, the principal subjects being Shakespeare and Walt's own *Leaves of Grass*. Over Shakespeare it was a sort of triangular combat—O'Connor maintaining the Baconian theory of the authorship of the plays, and Walt joining with me in attacking that chimera. On the other hand, I agreed with O'Connor in his estimate of Lear and Hamlet and Othello, which Walt belittled, preferring the historical plays, and placing Richard II foremost; although he thought all the plays preposterously overrated. Of his own poems ("pomes" he called them) he spoke modestly, listening with interest to frank criticisms of them (which he always had from me), and disclaiming the profound hidden meanings which O'Connor was inclined to read into some of them. Ordinarily inert and slow of speech, on occasions like this his large and generous nature became suffused with a magnificent glow, which gave one some idea of the heat and momentum that went to the making of his truly great poems; just as his sluggish moods seemed to account for so much of his labored, unleavened work.

O'Connor was a man of unfailing eloquence, whom it was always delightful to listen to, even when the rush of his enthusiasm carried him beyond the bounds of discretion, as it did in the Bacon-Shakespeare business. Whitman's reasoning powers were not remarkable; he did not impress me, then or at any time, as a great intellect; but he was original, intuitive, a seer, and his immense and genial personality gave an interest to everything he said. In my enjoyment of such high discourse, I forgot the cheerless garret, the stove in which there was no fire, the window that remained open (Walt was a "fresh-air fiend"), and my own freezing feet (we all kept on our overcoats). I also forgot that I was a guest at the great house across the quadrangle, and that I was unprovided with a latch key—a fact of which I was reminded with rather startling unpleasantness, when I left O'Connor at the foot of Walt's stairs, hurried to the Secretary's door, I know not how long after midnight, and found myself locked out. All was still and dark within, except that I could see a light left burning low for me in my own chamber, a tantalizing reminder of the comfort I had exchanged for the bleak, deserted streets. My embarrassment was relieved when I reflected that in those wild war times the Secretary was prepared to receive dispatches at any hour of the night. I rang boldly, as if I had been a messenger bearing tidings of a nation's fate. The vestibule gas was quickly turned up, and a sleepy-looking colored boy let me in.

Two mornings after this I went by appointment to call on Whitman in his garret. "Don't come before ten o'clock," he had warned me; and it was after ten when I mounted his three flights and knocked at the door of his room—his terrible room, as I termed it in notes taken at the time.

I found him partly dressed, and preparing his own breakfast. There was a fire in the sheet-iron stove—the open door showed a few coals— and he was cutting slices of bread from a baker's loaf with his jackknife, getting them ready for toasting. The smallest of tin teakettles simmering on the stove, a bowl and spoon, and a covered tin cup used as a teapot comprised, with the aforesaid useful jackknife, his entire outfit of visible housekeeping utensils. His sugar bowl was a brown paper bag. His butter plate was another piece of brown paper, the same coarse wrapping in which he had brought home his modest lump from the corner grocery. His cupboard was an oblong pine box, set up a few feet from the floor, open-ing outward, with the bottom against the wall; the two sides, one above the other, made very good shelves.

I toasted his bread for him on the end of a sharpened stick; he but-tered the slices with his jackknife, and poured his tea at a corner of the table cleared for that purpose of its litter of books and newspapers; and while he breakfasted we talked.

His last slice buttered and eaten, he burned his butter plate (showing the advantage of having no dishes to wash), and set his bag of sugar in the cupboard, along with his small parcel of tea; then he brought out from his trunk a package of manuscript poems, which he read to me, and which we discussed, for the next hour.

These were his war pieces, the "Drum Taps," then nearly ready for publication. He read them unaffectedly, with force and feeling, and in a voice of rich but not resonant tones. I was interested not alone in the poems, but also in his own interpretation of the irregular yet often not unrhythmical lines. I did not find in them anything comparable with the greatly moving passages in the earlier *Leaves*: they were more literary in their tone, showing here and there lapses into the conventional poetic diction, which he had flung off so haughtily in the surge of the early impulse. They contained, however, some fine, effective, patriotic, and pathetic chants; and were, moreover, entirely free from the old offenses against propriety. I hoped to be able to persuade some good Boston house to publish the volume, but found, when I came to make the attempt, that no firm would undertake it; and it remained in manuscript until 1865, when Whitman issued it at his own expense. From that morning, I saw him almost every day or evening as long as I remained in Washington. He was then engaged in his missionary work in the hospitals; talking to the sick and wounded soldiers, reading to them, writing letters for them, cheering and comforting them sometimes by merely sitting silent beside their cots, and perhaps soothing a pallid brow with his sympathetic hand.

He took me two or three times to the great Armory Square Hospital, where I observed his methods of work. I was surprised to learn that he never read to the patients any of his own compositions, and that not one of those I talked with knew him for a poet, or for anybody but plain "Mr. Whitman." I cannot help speaking of one poor fellow, who had asked to see me because Whitman had told him I was the author of one of the pieces he liked to hear read, and who talked to me with tears in his eyes of the comfort Whitman's visits had given him. The pathos of the situation was impressed upon me by the circumstances that his foot was to be amputated within an hour.

Whitman always carried into the wards a few fruits and delicacies, which he distributed with the approval of the surgeons and nurses. He also circulated, among those who were well enough to read, books and periodicals sent to him for that purpose by friends in the North. Sometimes he gave paper and envelopes and postage stamps, and he was never without some good tobacco, to be dispensed in special cases. He never used tobacco himself, but he had compassion for those who had been deprived of that solace, as he had for all forms of suffering. He wrote Washington letters that winter for the New York Times, the income from which, together with contributions from Northern friends, enabled him to carry on his hospital work.

Whitman and Chase were the two men I saw most of, at that time, in Washington. I saw Chase daily, at his own table, with his friends and distinguished guests, and had many long walks and talks with him, when we took our morning exercise together before breakfast. That I should know them both familiarly, passing often from the stately residence of the one to the humble lodging of the other, seemed to me a simple and natural thing at the time; it appears much less simple to me now. Great men both, each nobly proportioned in body and stalwart in character, and each invincibly true to his own ideals and purposes; near neighbors, and yet very antipodes in their widely contrasted lives. Once princely in his position, the slenderest rill of which would have made life green for the other, struggling along the arid ways of an honorable poverty. Both greatly ambitious: Chase devoutly believing it his right, and likewise his destiny, to succeed Lincoln in the presidency; Whitman aspiring to be for all time the poet of democracy and emancipated manhood—his simple prayer being, "Give me to speak beautiful words; take all the rest!" One a conscientious High Churchman, reverencing tradition, and finding ceremonious worship so helpful and solacing that (as he once said to me earnestly) he would have become a Roman Catholic, if he could have brought himself to accept the Romish dogmas; the other believing in the immanent spirit and an ever living inspiration, and as free from all forms and doctrines as Abraham alone with the Deity in the desert. For the statesman I had a very great admiration and respect; for the poet I felt a powerful attraction, something like a younger brother's love; and I confess a sweet and secret joy in sometimes stealing away from the company of polished and eminent people in the great house, and crossing over to Walt in his garret, or going to meet him at O'Connor's.

I thought no man more than Whitman merited recognition and assistance from the government, and I once asked him if he would accept a position in one of the departments. He answered frankly that he would. But he believed it improbable that he could get an appointment, although (as he mentioned casually) he had letters of recommendation from Emerson.

There were two of these, and they were especially interesting to me, as I knew something of the disturbed relations existing between the two men, on account of Whitman's indiscreet use of Emerson's famous letter to him, acknowledging the gift copy of the first *Leaves of Grass*. Whitman not only published that letter without the writer's authority, but printed an

extract from it, in conspicuous gold, on the back of his second edition—
"I greet you at the beginning of a great career;" thus making Emerson in
some sense an indorser not only of the first poems, but of others he had
never seen, and which he would have preferred never to see in print. This
was an instance of bad taste, but not of intentional bad faith, on the part
of Whitman. Talking of it once, he said, in his grand way: "I supposed the
letter was meant to be blazoned; I regarded it as the chart of an emperor."
But Emerson had no thought of acting the imperial part toward so adven-
turous a voyager. I remember hearing him allude to the incident shortly
after that second edition appeared. Speaking of the attention the new poet
was attracting, he mentioned an Englishman who had come to this country bringing a letter to Whitman from Monckton Milnes (afterward Lord
Houghton). "But," said Emerson, "hearing that Whitman had not used me
well in the matter of letters, he did not deliver it." He had afterwards made
a strenuous effort to induce Whitman to omit certain objectionable passages from his edition of 1860, and failed. And I knew that the later writings of Whitman interested him less and less. "No more evidence of getting into form," he once remarked—a singular comment, it may be
though, from one whose own chief defect as a writer seemed to be an
imperfect mastery of form.

With these things in mind, I read eagerly the two letters from
Emerson recommending Whitman for a government appointment. One
was addressed to Senator Sumner; the other, I was surprised and pleased
to find, to Secretary Chase. I had but a slight acquaintance with Sumner,
and the letter to him I handed back. The one written to Chase I wished to
retain, in order to deliver it to the Secretary with my own hands, and with
such furthering words as I could summon in so good a cause. Whitman
expressed small hope in the venture, and stipulated that in case of the failure he anticipated I should bring back the letter.

As we left the breakfast table, the next morning, I followed the
Secretary into his private office, where, after some pleasant talk, I
remarked that I was about to overstep a rule I had laid down for myself
on entering his house. He said, "What rule?" I replied, "Never to repay
your hospitality by asking of you any official favor." He said I needn't have
thought it necessary to make that rule, for he was always glad to do for his
friends such things as he was constantly called upon to do for strangers.
Then I laid before him the Whitman business. He was evidently impressed
by Emerson's letter, and he listened with interest to what I had to say of

the man and his patriotic work. But he was troubled. "I am placed," he said, "in a very embarrassing position. It would give me great pleasure to grant this request, out of my regard to Mr. Emerson"; and he was gracious enough to extend the courtesy of this "regard" to me, also. But then he went on to speak of *Leaves of Grass* as a book that had made the author notorious; and I found that he judged it, as all but a very few persons then did, not independently, on its own epoch-making merits, but by conventional standards of taste and propriety. He had understood that the writer was a rowdy—"one of the roughs,"—according to his descriptions of himself.

I said, "He is as quiet a gentleman in his manners and conversation as any guest who enters your door." He replied: "I am bound to believe what you say; but his writings have given him a bad repute, and I should not know what sort of a place to give to such a man,"—with more to the same purpose.

I respected his decision, much as I regretted it; and, persuaded that nothing I could urge would induce him to change it, I said I would relieve him of all embarrassment in the business by withdrawing the letter. He glanced again at the signature, hesitated, and made this surprising response: "I have nothing of Emerson's in his handwriting, and I shall be glad to keep this."

I thought it hardly fair, but as the letter was addressed to him, and had passed into his hands, I couldn't well reclaim it against his wishes.

Whitman seemed really to have formed some hopes of the success of my mission, after I had undertaken it, as he showed when I went to give him an account of my interview with the Secretary. He took the disappointment philosophically, but indulged in some sardonic remarks regarding Chase and his department. "He is right," he said, "in preserving his saints from contamination by a man like me!" But I stood up for the Secretary, as, with the Secretary, I had stood up for Whitman. Could any one be blamed for taking the writer of *Leaves of Grass* at his word when, in his defiance of conventionality, he had described himself as "rowdyish," "disorderly," and worse? " 'I cock my hat as I please, indoors and out,' " I quoted. Walt laughed, and said, "I don't blame him; it's about what I expected." He asked for the letter, and showed his amused disgust when I explained how it had been pocketed by the Secretary.

I should probably have had no difficulty in securing the appointment if I had withheld Emerson's letter, and called my friend simply Mr.

Whitman, or Mr. Walter Whitman, without mentioning *Leaves of Grass*. But I felt that the Secretary, if he was to appoint him, should know just whom he was appointing; and Whitman was the last person in the world to shirk the responsibility of having written an audacious book.

Whether the same candor was used in procuring for him a clerkship in the Interior Department, to which he was appointed later, I do not know. He had been for some time performing the duties of that position, without exciting any other comment than that he performed them well, when a new Secretary, coming in under Johnson, and discovering that the grave and silent man at a certain desk was the author of a reprehensible book, dismissed him unceremoniously.

It was this incident that called out from O'Connor his brilliant monograph, The Good Gray Poet, in which Whitman was so eloquently vindicated, and the Secretary received so terrible a scourging. What seemed for a time unmitigated ill fortune proved to be a very good thing for Whitman. He was soon after appointed to a better place in the office of the Attorney-General, and he himself used to say that it was O'Connor's defense that turned the tide in his favor; meaning the tide of criticism and public opinion, which had until then set so tremendously against him. O'Connor's pamphlet was followed, two years later (1867), by John Burroughs's Walt Whitman as Poet and Person. Countless other publications on the same inexhaustible theme have appeared since—reviews, biographies, personal recollections, studies of Walt Whitman; a recent Study by Burroughs himself; volumes of eulogy and exegesis, commentary and controversy, wise and foolish; a whole library of Whitman literature, in English, French, German, and other languages. There are Walt Whitman Societies and Fellowships, and at least one periodical is devoted mainly to Whitmanana.

I saw Whitman many times in Washington, after that memorable season of 1863; again when he came to Boston to deliver his lecture on Lincoln; and lastly in his Camden home, where the feet of many pilgrims mounted the steps that led to his door, and where an infirm but serene old age closed the "great career" Emerson had been the first to acclaim.

All this time I have watched with deep interest the growth of his influence and the change in public opinion regarding him. To me, now almost the sole survivor among his earliest friends and adherents, wonderful indeed seems that change since the first thin quarto edition of the *Leaves* appeared, in 1855. If noticed at all by the critics, it was, with rare exceptions, to be ridiculed and reviled; and Emerson himself suffered abuse for pronouncing it "the most extraordinary piece of wit and wisdom America had yet contributed." Even so accomplished a man of letters as James Russell Lowell saw in it nothing but commonplace tricked out with eccentricity. I remember walking with him once in Cambridge, when he pointed out a doorway sign, "Groceries," with the letters set zigzag, to produce a bizarre effect. "That," said he, "is Walt Whitman—with very common goods inside." It was not until his writings became less prophetical, and more consciously literary in their aim, that Lowell and scholars of his class began to see something besides oddity in Whitman, and his popularity widened.

That such a change took place in his writings Whitman himself was aware. Once when I confessed to him that nothing in the later poems moved me like some of the great passages in the earlier editions, he replied: "I am not surprised. I do not suppose I shall ever again have the afflatus I had in writing the first *Leaves of Grass*." One evening he was reading to O'Connor and me some manuscript pieces, inviting our comments, when he came to the line—"No poem proud I, chanting, bring to thee."

"Why do you say 'poem proud'?" I asked. "You never would have said that in the first *Leaves of Grass*."

"What would I have said?" he inquired.

" 'I bring to you no proud poem,' " I replied.

O'Connor cried out, in his vehement way, "That's so, Walt—that's so!"

"I think you are right," Walt admitted, and he read over the line, which I looked to see changed when the poem came to be printed; but it appeared without alteration. It occurs in Lo, Victress on the Peaks, an address to Liberty, for which word he uses the Spanish "Libertad,"—another thing with which I found fault, and which I hoped to see changed. I will say here that I do not believe Whitman ever changed a line or a word to please anybody. In answer to criticism, he would sometimes maintain his point; at others, he would answer, in his tolerant, candid way, "I guess you are right," or, "I rather think it is so;" but even when apparently convinced, he would stand by his faults. His use of words and phrases from foreign languages, which he began in his 1856 edition, and which became a positive offense in that of 1860, he continued in the face of all remonstrance, and would not even correct errors into which his ignorance of those languages had betrayed him. In one of his most ambitious poems, Chanting the Square Deific, he translates our good English "Holy Spirit" into "Santa Spirita," meant for Italian; but in that language the word for "spirit" is masculine, and the form should have been "Spirito Santo," with the adjective correspondingly masculine. William Rossetti, who edited a volume of selections from *Leaves of Grass* for the British public, pointed this out in a letter to Whitman, who, in talking of it with me, acknowledged the blunder; yet through some perversity he allowed it to pass on into subsequent editions.

In these editions Whitman showed that he was not averse to making changes; he was always rearranging the contents, mixing up the early with the later poems, and altering titles, to the confusion of the faithful. Now and then he would interject into some familiar passage of the old pieces a phrase or a line in his later manner, strangely discordant to an ear of any discrimination. A good example is this, where to the original lines—"My rendezvous is appointed, it is certain,/ The Lord will be there, and wait till I come, on perfect terms"—he adds this third line—"The great Camerado, the lover true for whom I pine, will be there"—a tawdry patch on the strong original homespun. The French "rendezvous" in the first line is legitimate, having been adopted into our language because it expresses something for which we have no other single word, and Whitman would be a benefactor had he enriched our vernacular in that way. but "camerado"—of which he seems to have become very fond, using it wherever he had a chance—is neither French (camarade) nor Spanish (camarada), nor anything else, to my mind, but a malformed substitute for our good and sufficient word "comrade." "Lover true," like "poem proud," is of a piece with those "stock poetical touches" which he used to say he had great trouble in leaving out of his first *Leaves*, but which here, as in other places, he went back and deliberately wrote into them.

For another set of changes to which I objected he was able to give a reason, though a poor one. In the Poem of Faces, "the old face of the mother of many children" has this beautiful setting:

> "Lulled and late is the smoke of the Sabbath morning,
> It hangs low over the rows of trees by the fences,
> It hangs thin by the sassafras, the wild cherry, and the
> cat-brier under them."

"Smoke of the Sabbath morning" he altered, after the first two editions, to "smoke of the First Day morning." In like manner, elsewhere, "the field-sprouts of April and May" was changed to "the field-sprouts of Fourth Month and Fifth Month"; "the short last daylight of December" to "the short last daylight of "Twelfth Month," and so on—all our good old pagan names for the months and days, wherever they occurred in the original *Leaves*, being reduced to numbers, in plain Quaker fashion, or got rid of in some other way. "I mind how we lay in June" became "I mind how we once lay;" and "The exquisite, delicate-thin curve of the new moon in May"—a most exquisite and delicate line, it may be observed in passing—was made to read, not "new moon in Fifth Month" (that would have been a little too bad), but "new moon in spring." I thought all of these alterations unfortunate, except perhaps the last; nearly all involving a sacrifice of euphony or of atmosphere in the lines. When I remonstrated against what seemed an affectation, he told me that he was brought up among Quakers; but I considered that too narrow a ground for the throwing out of words in common use among all English-speaking peoples except a single sect. To my mind, it was another proof that in matters of taste and judgment he was extremely fallible, and capable of doing unwise and wayward things for the sake of a theory or of a caprice.

In one important particular he changed, if not his theory, at least his practice. After the edition of 1860 he became reserved upon the one subject tabooed in polite society, the free treatment of which he had declared essential to his scheme of exhibiting in his poems humanity entire and undraped. For just six years, from 1855 to 1860 only, he illustrated that theory with arrogant defiance; then no further exemplifications of it appeared in all his prose and verse for more than thirty years, or as long as he continued to write. It was a sudden and significant, change, which was, however, covered from observation in the reshuffling of the *Leaves*. In thus re-editing the earlier poems, he quietly dropped out a few of the most startling lines, and would, I believe, have canceled many more, but his pride was adamant to anything that seemed a concession.

No doubt Whitman suffered some impairment of his mental faculties in the long years of his invalidism. He is said to have gone over to the Bacon side of the Bacon-Shakespeare controversy, and even to have accepted the Donnelly cipher. How confused his memory became on one subject of paramount interest is evinced by a passage in his Backward Glance o'er Travel'd Roads, where he says of the beginnings of *Leaves of Grass* that, although he had "made a start before," all might have come to naught—"almost positively would have come to naught"—but for the stimulus he received from the "sights and scenes" of the secession war. To make this more emphatic, he adds the astounding assertion, "Without those three or four years [1862 to 1865], and the experiences they gave, *Leaves of Grass* would not now be existing." Whereas he had only to look at his title-pages to see that not his first, nor his second, but his third edition, comprising the larger and by far the most important part of his poetic work, was published in 1860, months before the first gun of the war was fired or a single state had seceded. After this, we need not wonder that he forgot he had read Emerson before writing his first *Leaves*.

When Whitman's genius flows, his unhampered lines suit his purposes as no other form of verse could do. The thought is sometimes elusive, hiding in metaphor and suggestion, but the language is direct, idiomatic, swift, its torrent force and copiousness justifying his disregard of rhyme and metre; indeed, it has often a wild, swinging rhythm of its own. But when no longer impelled by the stress of meaning and emotion, it becomes strained and flavorless, an, at its worst, involved, parenthetical, enfeebled by weak inversions.

There are the same disturbing inequalities in his prose as in his verse. The preface to his first edition exhibits the masterful characteristics of his great poems; indeed, much of that preface made very good *Leaves*, when he afterwards rewrote it in lines and printed it as poetry. At its worst, his prose is lax and slovenly, or it takes on ruggedness to simulate strength, and jars and jolts like a farm wagon on stony roads. Some of his published letters are slipshod in their composition, and in their disregard of capitalization and punctuation, almost to the verge of illiteracy. Had William Shakespeare left any authentic writings as empty of thought and imagination, and void of literary value, as some of the Calamus letters, they would have afforded a better argument that any we now have against his authorship of the plays. Perhaps some future tilter at windmills will attempt to prove that the man we know as Walt Whitman was an uncultured impostor, who had obtained possession of a mass of powerful but fragmentary writings by some unknown man of genius, which he exploited, pieced together, and mixed up with compositions of his own.

But after all deductions it remains to be unequivocally affirmed that Whitman stands as a great original force in our literature; perhaps one of the greatest. Art, as exemplified by such poets as Longfellow and Tennyson, he has little or none; but in the free play of his power he produces the effect of an art beyond art. His words are often steeped in the very sentiment of the themes they touch, and suggest more than they express. He has largeness of view, an all-including optimism, boundless love and faith. To sum all in a sentence, I should say that his main purpose was to bring into his poems Nature, with unflinching realism—especially Nature's living masterpiece, Man; and to demonstrate that everything in Nature and in Man, all that he is, feels, and observes, is worthy of celebration by the poet; not in the old, selective, artificial poetic forms, but with a freedom of method commensurate with Nature's own amplitude and unconstraint. It was a grand conception, an intrepid revolt against the established canons of taste and art, a challenge and a menace to the greatest and most venerated names. That the attempt was not so foolhardy as at first appeared, and that it has not been altogether a failure, the growing interest in the man and his work sufficiently attests; and who can say how greatly it might have succeeded, if adequate judgment had reinforced his genius, and if his inspiration had continued as long as he continued to write?

The Atlantic Monthly
February 1902; REMINISCENCES OF WALT WHITMAN
Volume 89, No. 2; pages 163–175.

Selected Poems

Leaves of Grass

✴

Starting from the Paumanok

Starting from fish-shape Paumanok where I was born,
Well-begotten, and rais'd by a perfect mother,
After roaming many lands, lover of populous pavements,
Dweller in Mannahatta my city, or on southern savannas,
Or a soldier camp'd or carrying my knapsack and gun, or a miner in
    California,
Or rude in my home in Dakota's woods, my diet meat, my drink from
    the spring,
Or withdrawn to muse and meditate in some deep recess,
Far from the clank of crowds intervals passing rapt and happy,
Aware of the fresh free giver the flowing Missouri, aware of mighty
    Niagara,
Aware of the buffalo herds grazing the plains, the hirsute and strong-
    breasted bull,
Of earth, rocks, Fifth-month flowers experienced, stars. rain, snow,
    my amaze,
Having studied the mocking-bird's tones and the flight of the mountain-
    hawk,
And heard at dusk the unrivall'd one, the hermit thrush from the
    swamp-cedars,
Solitary, singing in the West, I strike up for a New World.

Song of Myself

I celebrate myself, and sing myself,
And what I assume you shall assume,
For every atom belonging to me as good belongs to you.

I loafe and invite my soul,
I lean and loafe at my ease observing a spear of summer grass.

My tongue, every atom of roy blood, forrn'd from this soil, this air,
Born here of parents born here from parents the same, and their parents
    the same,
I, now thirty-seven years old in perfect health begin,
Hoping to cease not till death.

Creeds and schools in abeyance,
Retiring back a while sufficed at what they are, but never forgotten,
I harbor for good or bad, I permit to speak at every hazard,
Nature without check with original energy.

2

Have you reckon'd a thousand acres much? have you reckon'd the
    earth much?
Have you practis'd so long to learn to read?
Have you felt so proud to get at the meaning of poems?

Stop this day and night with me and you shall possess the origin of all
    poems,
You shall possess the good of the earth and sun (there are millions of
    suns left),
You shall no longer take things at second or third hand, nor look
    through the eyes of the dead, nor feed on the spectres in books,
You shall not look through my eyes either, nor take things from me,
You shall listen to all sides and filter them from your self.

6

A child said *What is the grass?* fetching it to me with full hands;
How could I answer the child? I do not know what it is any more than he.

I guess it must be the flag of my disposition, out of hopeful green
    stuff woven.

Or I guess it is the handkerchief of the Lord, A scented gift and
    remembrancer designedly dropt,
Bearing the owner's name someway in the corners, that we may see and
    remark, and say *Whose?*

Or I guess the grass is itself a child, the produced babe of the vegetation.

Or I guess it is a uniform hieroglyphic,
And it means, Sprouting alike in broad zones and narrow zones,
Growing among black folks as among white,

Kanuck, Tuckahoe, Congressman, Cuff, I give them the same, I receive
    them the same.

And now it seems to me the beautiful uncut hair of graves.

Tenderly will I use you curling grass,
It may be you transpire from the breasts of young men,
It may be if I had known them I would have loved them,
It may be you are from old people, or from offspring taken soon out of
    their mothers' laps,
And here you are the mothers' laps.

This grass is very dark to be from the white heads of old mothers,
Darker than the colorless beards of old men,
Dark to come from under the faint red roofs of mouths.

O I perceive after all so many uttering tongues,
And I perceive they do not come from the roofs of mouths
    for nothing.

I wish I could translate the hints about the dead young men and women,
And the hints about old men and mothers, and the offspring taken soon
    out of their laps.

What do you think has become of the young and old men?
And what do you think has become of the women and children?

They are alive and well somewhere,
The smallest sprout shows there is really no death,
And if ever there was it led forward life, and does not wait
    at the end to arrest it,
And ceas'd the moment life appear'd.
All goes onward and outward, nothing collapses,
And to die is different from what any one supposed, and
    luckier.

10

Alone far in the wilds and mountains I hunt,
Wandering amazed at my own lightness and glee,
In the late afternoon choosing a safe spot to pass the night,
Kindling a fire and broiling the fresh-kill'd game,
Falling asleep on the gather'd leaves with my dog and gun by my side.

The Yankee clipper is under her sky-sails, she cuts the sparkle and scud,
My eyes settle the land, I bend at her prow or shout joyously from the deck.

The boatmen and clam-diggers arose early and stopt for me, I tuck'd my
    trowser-ends in my boots and went and had a
    good time;
You should have been with us that day round the chowder kettle.

I saw the marriage of the trapper in the open air in the far west, the
    bride was a red girl,
Her father and his friends sat near cross-legged and dumbly smoking,
    they had moccasins to their feet and large thick blankets hanging
    from their shoulders,
On a bank lounged the trapper, he was drest mostly in skins, his
    luxuriant beard and curls protected his neck, he held his bride by

the hand,
She had long eyelashes, her head was bare, her coarse straight locks
    descended upon her voluptuous limbs and reach'd to her feet.

The runaway slave came to my house and stopt outside,
I heard his motions crackling the twigs of the woodpile,
Through the swung half-door of the kitchen I saw him limpsy and weak,
And went where he sat on a log and led him in and assured him,
And brought water and fihl'd a tub for his sweated body and bruis'd feet,
And gave him a room that enter'd from my own, and gave him some
    coarse clean clothes,
And remember perfectly well his revolving eyes and his awkwardness,
And remember putting plasters on the galls of his neck and ankles;
He staid with me a week before he was recuperated and pass'd north,
I had him sit next me at table, my fire-lock lean'd in the corner.

13

The negro holds firmly the reins of his four horses, the
    block swags underneath on its tied-over chain,
The negro that drives the long dray of the stone-yard,
    steady and tall he stands pois'd on one leg on the string-piece,
His blue shirt exposes his ample neck and breast and
    loosens over his hip-band,
His glance is calm and commanding, he tosses the slouch
    of his hat away from his forehead,
The sun falls on his crispy hair and mustache, falls on the
    black of his polish'd and perfect limbs.

I behold the picturesque giant and love him, and I do not stop there,
I go with the team also.

In me the caresser of life wherever moving, backward as well as forward
    sluing,
To niches aside and junior bending, not a person or object missing,
Absorbing all to myself and for this song.

Oxen that rattle the yoke and chain or halt in the leafy shade, what is
    that you express in your eyes?

It seems to me more than all the print I have read in my life.

My tread scares the wood-drake and wood-duck on my distant and day-
    long ramble,
They rise together, they slowly circle around.

I believe in those wing'd purposes,
And acknowledge red, yellow, white, playing within me,
And consider green and violet and the tufted crown intentional,
And do not call the tortoise unworthy because she is not something else,
And the jay in the woods never studied the gamut, yet trills pretty well
        to me,
And the look of the bay mare shames silliness out of me.

I am of old and young, of the foolish as much as the wise,
Regardless of others, ever regardful of others,
Maternal as well as paternal, a child as well as a man.
Stuff'd with the stuff that is coarse and stuff'd with the stuff that is fine,
One of the Nation of many nations, the smallest the same and the largest
        the same,
A Southerner soon as a Northerner, a planter nonchalant and hospitable
        down by the Oconee I live,
A Yankee bound my own way ready for trade, my joints the limberest
        joints an earth and the sternest joints on earth,
A Kentuckian walking the vale of the Elkhorn in my deerskin leggings, a
        Louisianian or Georgian,
A boatman over lakes or bays or along coasts, a Hoosier, Badger,
        Buckeye;
At home on Kanadian snow-shoes or up in the bush, or with fishermen off
        Newfoundland,
At home in the fleet of ice-boats, sailing with the rest and tacking,
At home on the hills of Vermont or in the woods of Maine,
        or the Texan ranch,
Comrade of Californians, comrade of free North-Westerners, (loving
        their big proportions)
Comrade of raftsmen and coalmen, comrade of all who shake hands and
        welcome to drink and meat,
A learner with the simplest, a teacher of the thoughtfullest,
A novice beginning yet experient of myriads of seasons,

Of every hue and caste am I, of every rank and religion,
A farmer, mechanic, artist, gentleman, sailor, quaker,
Prisoner, fancy-man, rowdy, lawyer, physician, priest.

I resist any thing better than my own diversity,
Breathe the air but leave plenty after me,
And am not stuck up, and am in my place.
(The moth and the fish-eggs are in their place,
The bright suns I see and the dark suns I cannot see are in their place,
The palpable is in its place and the impalpable is in its place.)

17

These are really the thoughts of all men in all ages and lands, they are not
    original with me,
If they are not yours as much as mine they are nothing, or next to nothing,
If they are not the riddle and the untying of the riddle they are nothing,
If they are not just as close as they are distant they are nothing.
This is the grass that grows wherever the land is and the water is,
This the common air that bathes the globe.

21

I am the poet of the Body and I am the poet of the Soul,
The pleasures of heaven are with me and the pains of hell
    are with me,
The first I graft and increase upon myself, the latter I translate into a
    new tongue.

I am the poet of the woman the same as the man,
And I say it is as great to be a woman as to be a man,
And I say there is nothing greater than the mother of men.

I chant the chant of dilation or pride,
We have had ducking and deprecating about enough,
I show that size is only development.

Have you outstript the rest? are you the President?
It is a trifle, they will more than arrive there every one, and still pass on.

I am he that walks with the tender and growing night I call to the earth
and sea half-held by the night.

Press close bare-bosom'd night—press close magnetic nourishing night!
Night of south winds—night of the large few stars!
Still nodding night—mad naked summer night.

Smile O voluptuous cool-breath'd earth!
Earth of the slumbering and liquid trees
Earth of departed sunset—earth of the mountains mistytopt!
Earth of the vitreous pour of the full moon just tinged with blue!
Earth of shine and dark mottling the tide of the river!
Earth of the limpid gray of clouds brighter and clearer for my sake
Far-swooping elbow'd earth—rich apple-blossom'd earth Smile, for your
lover comes.

Prodigal, you have given me love—therefore I to you give love!
O unspeakable passionate love.

23

Endless unfolding of words of ages!
And mine a word of the modern, the word En-Masse.
A word of the faith that never balks,
Here or henceforward it is all the same to me, I accept Time absolutely.

It alone is without flaw, it alone rounds and completes all,
That mystic baffling wonder alone completes all.

I accept Reality and dare not question it,
Materialism first and last imbuing.
Hurrah for positive science long live exact demonstration!
Fetch stonecrop mixt with cedar and branches of lilac,
This is the lexicographer, this the chemist, this made a grammar of the
old cartouches,
These mariners put the ship through dangerous unknown seas,
This is the geologist, this works with the scalpel, and this is a
mathematician.

Gentlemen, to you the first honors always!
Your facts are useful, and yet they are not my dwelling,
I but enter by them to an area of my dwelling.

Less the reminders of properties told my words, And more the
    reminders they of life untold, and of freedom and extrication.

32

I think I could turn and live with animals, they are so placid and self-
    coatain'd,
I stand and look at them long and long.
They do sweat and whine about their condition,
They do not lie awake in the dark and weep for their sins,
They do not make me sick discussing their duty to God,
Not one is dissatisfied, not one is demented with the mania of owning
    things,
Not one kneels to another, nor to his kind that lived thousands of
    years ago,
Not one is respectable or unhappy over the whole earth.

So they show their relations to me and I accept them,
They bring me tokens of myself, they evince them plainly in their
    possession.

I wonder where they get those tokens,
Did I pass that wayhuge times ago and negligently drop them?
Myself moving forward then and now and forever,
Gathering and showing more always and with velocity,
Infinite and omnigenous, and the like of these among them,
Not too exclusive toward the reachers of my remembrancers,
Picking out here one that I love, and now go with him on brotherly terms.

A gigantic beauty of a stallion, fresh and responsive to my caresses,
Head high in the forehead, wide between the ears,
Limbs glossy and supple, tail dusting the ground,
Eyes full of sparkling wickedness, ears finely cut, flexibly moving.

His nostrils dilate as my heels embrace him,

His well-built limbs tremble with pleasure as we race around and return.

I but use you a minute, then I resign you, stallion,
Why do I need your paces when I myself out-gallop them?
Even as I stand or sit passing faster than you.

33

I understand the large hearts of heroes,
The courage of present times and all times,
How the skipper saw the crowded and rudderless wreck of the
      steamship, and Death chasing it up and down the
      storm,
How he knuckled tight and gave not back an inch, and was faithful of
      days and faithful of nights,
And chalk'd in large letters on a board, Be of good cheer, we will not
      desert you;
How he follow'd with them and tack'd with them three days and would
      not give it up,
How he saved the drifting company at last,
How the lank loose-gown'd women look'd when boated from the side of
      their prepared graves,
How the silent old-faced infants and the lifted sick, and the sharp-lipp'd
      unshaved men;
All this I swallow, it tastes good, I like it well, it becomes
      mine,
I am the man, I suffer'd, I was there.

The disdain and calmness of martyrs,
The mother of old, condemn'd for a witch, burnt with dry wood, her
      children gazing on,
The hounded slave that flags in the race, leans by the fence,
blowing, cover'd with sweat,
The twinges that sting like needles his legs and neck, the murderous
      buckshot and the bullets,
All these I feel or am.

I am the hounded slave, I wince at the bite of the dogs,
Hell and despair are upon me, crack and again crack the marksmen.

I clutch the rails of the fence, my gore dribs, thinn'd with the ooze of
    my skin,
I fall on the weeds and stones,
The riders spur their unwilling horses, haul close,
Taunt my dizzy ears and beat me violently over the head
   with whip-stocks.

Agonies are one of my changes of garments,
I do not ask the wounded person how he feels,
I myself become the wounded person,
My hurts turn livid upon me as I lean on a cane and observe.

I am the mash'd fireman with breast-bone broken,
Tumbling walls buried me in their debris,
Heat and smoke I inspired, I heard the yelling shouts of my comrades,
I heard the distant click of their picks and shovels,
They have clear'd the beams away, they tenderly lilt me forth.

I lie in the night air in my red shirt, the pervading hush is for joy sake,
Painless after all I lie exhausted but not so unhappy,
White and beautiful are the faces around me, the heads are bared of
    their fire-caps,
The kneeling crowd fades with the light of the torches.

Distant aid dead resuscitate,
They show as the dial or move as the hands of rue, I am the clock
    myself.

I am an old artillerist, I tell of my fort's bombardment,
I am there again.
Again the long roll of the drummers,
Again the attacking cannon, mortars,
Again to my listening ears the cannon responsive.

I take part, I see and hear the whole,
The cries, curses, roar, the plaudits for well-aim'd shots,
The ambulanza slowly passing trailing its red drip,
Workmen searching after damages, making indispensable repairs,
The fall of grenades through the rent roof, the fan-shaped explosion,

The whizz of limbs, heads, stone, wood, iron, high in the air.

Again gurgles the mouth of my dying general, he furiously waves with
    his hand,
He gasps through the clot *Mind not me—mind—the entrenchments.*

35

Would you hear of an old-time sea-fight?
Would you learn who won by the light of the moon and stars?
List to the yarn, as my grandmother's father the sailor told it to me.

Our foe was no skulk in his ship I tell you, (said he)
His was the surly English pluck, and there is no tougher or truer, and
    never was, and never will be;
Along the lower'd eve he came horribly raking us.

We closed with him, the yards entangled, the cannon touch'd,
My captain lash'd fast with his own hands.
We had receiv'd some eighteen pound shots under the water,
On our lower-gun-deck two large pieces had burst at the first fire, killing
    all around and blowing up overhead.

Fighting at sun-down, fighting at dark,
Ten o'clock at night, the full moon well up, our leaks on the gain, and
    five feet of water reported,
The master-at-arms loosing the prisoners confined in the after-hold to
    give them a chance for themselves.

The transit to and from the magazine is now stopt by the sentinels,
They see so many strange faces they do not know whom to trust.

Our frigate takes fire, The other asks if we demand quarter?
If our colors are struck and the fighting done?

Now I laugh content, for I hear the voice of my little captain,
We have not struck, he composedly cries, *we have just begun our part of the
    fighting.*

Only three guns are in use,
One is directed by the captain himself against the enemy's mainmast,
Two well serv'd with grape and canister silence his musketry and clear
    his decks.

The tops alone second the fire of this little battery, especially the main-
    top,
They hold out bravely during the whole of the action.

Not a moment's cease,
The leaks gain fast on the pumps, the fire eats toward the powder-magazine.

One of the pumps has been shot away, it is generally thought we are
    sinking.

Serene stands the little captain,
He is not hurried, his voice is neither high nor low,
His eyes give more light to us than our battle lanterns.

Toward twelve there in the beams of the moon they surrender to us.

40

To any one dying, thither I speed and twist the knob of the door,
Turn the bed-clothes toward the foot of the bed,
Let the physician and the priest go home.

I seize the descending man and raise him with resistless will,
O despairer, here is my neck,
By God, you shall not go down! hang your whole weight upon me.

I dilate you with tremendous breath, I buoy you up,
Every room of the house do I fill with an arm'd force,
Lovers of me, bafflers of grave,
Sleep—I and they keep guard all night,
Not doubt, not decease shall dare to lay finger upon you,
I have embraced you, and henceforth possess you to myself,
And when you rise in the morning you will find what I tell you is so.

44

Long I was hugg'd close—long and long.

Immense have been the preparations for me,
Faithful and friendly the arms that have help'd me.

Cycles ferried my cradle, rowing and rowing like cheerful boatmen,
For room to me stars kept aside in their own rings,
They sent influences to look after what was to hold me.

Before I was born out of my mother generations guided me,
My embryo has never been torpid, nothing could overlay it.

For it the nebula cohered to an orb,
The long slow strata piled to rest it on,
Vast vegetables gave it sustenance,
Monstrous sauroids transported it in their mouths and deposited it
    with care.

All forces have been steadily employ'd to complete and delight me,
Now on this spot I stand with my robust soul.

45

Old age supe'rbly rising! O welcome, ineffable grace of dying days!
Every condition promulges not only itself, it promulges what grows after
    and out of itself,
And the dark hush promulges as much as any.

I open my scuttle at night and see the far-sprinkled systems,
And all I see multiplied as high as I can cipher edge but the rim of the
    farther systems.

Wider and wider they spread, expanding, always expanding,
Outward and outward and forever outward.

My sun has his sun and round him obediently wheels,
He joins with his partners a group of superior circuit,

And greater sets follow, making specks of the greatest inside them.

There is no stoppage and never can be stoppage,
If I, you, and the worlds, and all beneath or upon their surfaces, were
    this moment reduced back to a pallid float, it would not avail in the
    long run,
We should surely bring up again where we now stand,
And surely go as much farther, and then farther and
    farther.

A few quadrillions of eras, a few octill ions of cubic leagues,
    do not hazard the span or make it impatient,
They are but parts, any thing is but a part.
See ever so far, there is limitless space outside of that,
Count ever so much, there is limitless time around that.

My rendezvous is appointed, it is certain,
    The Lord will be there and wait till I come on perfect terms,
The great Camerado, the lover true for whom I pine will be there.

48

I have said that the soul is not more than the body,
And I have said that the body is not more than the soul,
And nothing, not God, is greater to one than one's self is,
And whoever walks a furlong without sympathy walks to
    his own funeral drest in his shroud,
And I or you pocketless of a dime may purchase the pick of the earth,
And to glance with an eye or show a bean in its pod confounds the
    learning of all times.
And there is no trade or employment but the young man following it
    may become a hero,
And there is no object so soft but it makes a hub for the wheel'd
    universe,
And I say any man or woman, Let your soul stand cool and composed
    before a million universes.

And I say to mankind, Be not curious about God,
For I who am curious about each am not curious about God,

(No array of terms can say how much I am at peace about
God and about death.)
I hear and behold God in every object, yet understand God not in
the least,
Nor do I understand who there can be more wonderful than myself.

Why should I wish to see God better than this day?
I see something of God each hour of the twenty-four, and each
moment then,
In the faces of men and women I see God, and in my own face in the glass,
I find letters from God dropt in the street, and every one is sign'd by
God's name,
And I leave them where they are, for I know that wheresoe'er I go,
Others will punctually come for ever and ever.

51

The past and present wilt—I have fill'd them, emptied them,
And proceed to fill my next fold of the future.

Listener up there! what have you to confide to me?
Look in my face while I snuff the sidle of evening, (Talk honestly, no one
else hears you, and I stay only a minute longer.)

Do I contradict myself?
Very well then I contradict myself,
(I am large, I contain multitudes.)

I concentrate toward them that are nigh, I wait on the door slab.
Who has done his day's work? who will soonest be through with his
supper?
Who wishes to walk with me?

Will you speak before I am gone? will you prove already too late?

52

The spotted hawk swoops by and accuses me, he complains of my gab
and my loitering.

I too am not a bit tamed, I too am untranslatable,
I sound my barbaric yawp over the roofs of the world.

The last scud of day holds back for me,
It flings my likeness after the rest and true as any on the shadow'd wilds,
It coaxes me to the vapor and the dusk.

I depart as air, I shake my white locks at the runaway sun,
I effuse my flesh in eddies, and drift it in lacy jags.

I bequeath myself to the dirt to grow from the grass I love,
If you want me again look for me under your boot-soles.

You will hardly know who I am or what I mean,
But I shall be good health to you nevertheless,
And filter and fibre your blood.

Failing to fetch me at first keep encouraged,
Missing me one place search another,
I stop somewhere waiting for you.

Mannahatta

I was asking for something specific and perfect for my city,
Whereupon lo! upsprang the aboriginal name.

Now I see what there is in a name, a word, liquid, sane, unruly, musical,
    self-sufficient,
I see that the word of my city is that word from of old,
Because I see that word nested in nests of water-bays,
    superb,
Rich, hemm'd thick all around with sailships and steamships, an island
    sixteen miles long, solid-founded,
Numberless crowded streets, high growths of iron, slender, strong, light,
    splendidly uprising toward clear skies,
Tides swift and ample, well-loved by me, toward sundown,
The flowing sea-currents, the little islands, larger adjoining
    islands, the heights, the villas,
The countless masts, the white shore-steamers, the lighters, the ferry-
    boats, the black sea-steamers well-model'd,
The down-town streets, the jobbers' houses of business, the houses of
    business of the ship-merchants and money-brokers, the river-streets,
Immigrants arriving, fifteen or twenty thousand in a week,
The carts hauling goods, the manly race of drivers of horses, the brown-
    faced sailors,
The summer air, the bright sun shining, and the sailing clouds aloft,
The winter snows, the sleigh-bells, the broken ice in the river, passing
    along up or down with the flood-tide or ebb-tide,
The mechanics of the city, the masters, well-form'd, beautiful-faced,
    looking you straight in the eyes,
Trottoirs throng'd, vehicles, Broadway, the women, the shops and shows,
A million people—manners free and superb—open voices—
    hospitality—the most courageous and friendly young men,
City of hurried and sparkling waters! city of spires and masts!
City nested in bays! my city!

At Auction

A Man's body at auction,
(For before the war I often go to the slave-mart and watch the sale)
I help the auctioneer, the sloven does not half know his business.

Gentlemen look on this wonder,
Whatever the bids of the bidders they cannot be high enough for it,
For it the globe lay preparing quintillions of years without one animal
    or plant,
For it the revolving cycles truly and steadily roll'd.

In this head the all-baffling brain,
In it and below it the makings of heroes.

Examine these limbs, red, black, or white, they are cunning in tendon
    and nerve,
They shall be stript that you may see them.

Exquisite senses, life-lit eyes, pluck, volition,
Flakes of breast-muscle, pliant backbone and neck, flesh
    not flabby, good-sized arms and legs,
And wonders within there yet.

Within there runs blood,
The same old blood! the same red-running blood!
There swells and jets a heart, there all passions, desires, reachings,
    aspirations,
(Do you think they are not there because they are not express'd in
    parlors and lecture-rooms?)

This is not only one man, this the father of those who shall be fathers in
    their turns,
In him the start of populous states and rich republics,
Of him countless immortal lives with countless embodiments and
    enjoyments.

How do you know who shall come from the offspring of his offspring
    through the centuries?
(Who might you find you have come from yourself, if you could trace
    back through the centuries?)

A woman's body at auction,
She too is not only herself, she is the teeming mother of mothers,
She is the bearer of them that shall grow and be mates to the mothers.

Have you ever loved the body of a woman?
Have you ever loved the body of a man?
Do you not see that these are exactly the same to all in all nations and
    times all over the earth?

If any thing is sacred the human body is sacred,
And the glory and sweet of a man is the token of manhood untainted,
And in man or woman a clean, strong, firm-fibred body, is more beauti-
    ful than the most beautiful face.

Have you seen the fool that corrupted his own live body? or the fool
    that corrupted her own live body?
For they do not conceal themselves, and cannot conceal themselves.

Salut Au Monde!

O take my hand Walt Whitman!
Such gliding wonders! such sights and sounds!
Such join'd unended links, each hook'd to the next,
Each answering all, each sharing the earth with all.

What widens within you Walt Whitman?
What waves and soils exuding?
What climes? what persons and cities are here?
Who are the infants, some playing, some slumbering?
Who are the girls? who are the married women?
Who are the groups of old men going slowly with their arms about each
    other's necks?
What rivers are these? what forests and fruits are these? What are the
    mountains call'd that rise so high in the mists ?
What myriads of dwellings are they fill'd with dwellers?

2

Within me latitude widens, longitude lengthens,
Asia, Africa, Europe, are to the east—America is provided
    for in the west,
Banding the bulge of the earth winds the hot equator,
Curiously north and south turn the axis-ends,
Within me is the longest day, the sun wheels in slanting
    rings, it does not set for months,
Stretch'd in due time within me the midnight sun just rises above the
    horizon and sinks again,
Within me zones, seas, cataracts, forests, volcanoes, groups,
Malaysia, Polynesia, and the great West Indian islands.

3

What do you hear Walt Whitman?

I hear the workman singing and the farmer's wife singing,
I hear in the distance the sounds of children and of animals

early in the day,
I hear emulous shouts of Australians pursuing the wild horse,
I hear the Spanish dance with castanets in the chestnut shade, to the
    rebeck and guitar,
I hear continual echoes from the Thames,
I hear fierce French liberty songs,
I hear of the Italian boat-sculler the musical recitative of old poems,
I hear the locusts in Syria as they strike the grain and grass with the
    showers of their terrible clouds,
I hear the Coptic refrain toward sundown, pensively falling on the breast
    of the black venerable vast mother the Nile,
I hear the chirp of the Mexican muleteer, and the bells of the mule,
I hear the Arab muezzin calling from the top of the mosque,
I hear the Christian priests at the altars of their churches,
I hear the responsive base and soprano,
I hear the cry of the Cossack, and the sailor's voice putting to sea at Okotsk,
I hear the wheeze of the slave-coffle as the slaves march on,
    as the husky gangs pass on by two and threes, fasten'd together
    with wrist-chains and ankle-chains,
I hear the Hebrew reading his records and psalms,
I hear the rhythmic myths of the Greeks, and the strong legends of
    the Romans,
I hear the tale of the divine life and bloody death of the beautiful
    God the Christ,
I hear the Hindoo teaching his favorite pupil the loves, wars, adages,
    transmitted safely to this day from poets who wrote three thousand
    years ago.

My spirit has pass'd in compassion and determination around the
    whole earth,
I have look'd for equals and lovers and found them ready for me in
    all lands,
I think some divine rapport has equalized sue with them.

You vapors, I think I have risen with you, moved away to distant
    continents, and fallen down there, for reasons,
I think I have blown with you you winds;
You waters I have finger'd every shore with you,
I have run through what any river or strait of the globe has run through,

I have taken my stand on the bases of peninsulas and on the high
    embedded rocks, to cry thence:

Salut au monde!
What cities the light or warmth penetrates I penetrate those cities myself,
All islands to which birds wing their way I wing my way myself.

Toward you all, in America's name,
I raise high the perpendicular hand, I make the signal,
To remain after me in sight forever,
For all the haunts and homes of men.

The boatman singing what belongs to him in his boat, the deck-hand
    singing on the steamboat deck,
The shoemaker singing as he sits on his bench, the hatter singing as
    he stands,
The wood-cutter's song, the ploughboy's on his way in the morning, or
    at noon intermission or at sundown,
The delicious singing of the mother, or of the young wife
    at work, or of the girl sewing or washing,
Each singing what belongs to him or her and to none else,
The day what belongs to the day—at night the party of young fellows,
    robust, friendly,
Singing with open mouths their strong melodious songs.

Crossing Brooklyn Ferry

1

Flood-tide below me! I see you face to face!
Clouds of the west—sun there half an hour high—I see you also
    face to face.

Crowds of men and women attired in the usual costumes, how curious
    you are to me!
On the ferry-boats the hundreds and hundreds that cross, returning
    home, are more curious to me than you suppose,
And you that shall cross from shore to shore years hence are more to
    me, and more in my meditations, than you might suppose.

2

The impalpable sustenance of me from all things at all hours of the day,
The simple, compact, well-join'd scheme, myself disintegrated, every
    one disintegrated yet part of the scheme,
The similitudes of the past and those of the future,
The glories strung like beads on my smallest sights and hearings, on the
    walk in the street and the passage over the river,
The current rushing so swiftly and swimming with me far away,
The others that are to follow me, the ties between me and them,
The certainty of others, the life, love, sight, hearing of others.
Others will enter the gates of the ferry and cross from shore to shore,
Others will watch the run of the flood-tide,
Others will see the shipping of Manhattan north and west, and the
    heights of Brooklyn to the south and east,
Others will see the islands large and small;
Fifty years hence, others will see them as they cross, the sun half an
    hour high,
A hundred years hence, or ever so many hundred years hence, others
    will see them,
Will enjoy the sunset, the pouring-in of the flood-tide, the falling-back
    to the sea of the ebb-tide.

3

It avails not, time nor place—distance avails not,
I am with you, you men and women of a generation, or ever so many
    generations hence,
Just as you feel when you look on the river and sky, so I felt,
Just as any of you is one of a living crowd, I was one of a
    crowd,

Just as you are refresh'd by the gladness of the river and the bright flow,
    I was refresh'd,
Just as you stand and lean on the rail, yet hurry with the swift current, I
    stood yet was hurried,
Just as you look on the numberless masts of ships and the thick-stem-
    m'd pipes of steamboats, I look'd.

I too many and many a time cross'd the river of old,
Watched the Twelfth-month sea-gulls, saw them high in the air floating
    with motionless wings, oscillating their bodies,
Saw how the glistening yellow lit up parts of their bodies and left the
    rest in strong shadow,
Saw the slow-wheeling circles and the gradual edging toward the south,
Saw the reflection of the summer sky in the water,
Had my eyes dazzled by the shimmering track of beams,
Look'd at the fine centrifugal spokes of light round the shape of my
    head in the sunlit water,
Look'd on the haze on the hills southward and south-westward,
Look'd on the vapor as it flew in fleeces tinged with violet,
Look'd toward the lower bay to notice the vessels arriving,
Saw their approach, saw aboard those that were near me,
Saw the white sails of schooners and sloops, saw the ships at anchor,
The sailors at work in the rigging or out astride the spars,
The round masts, the swinging motion of the hulls, the slender
    serpentine pennants,
The large and small steamers in motion, the pilot in their pilot-houses,
The white wake left by the passage, the quick tremulous whirl of the
    wheels,
The flags of all nations, the falling of them at sunset,

The scallop-edged waves in the twilight, the ladled cups, the frolicsome
    crests and glistening,
The stretch afar growing dimmer and dimmer, the gray walls of the
    granite storehouses by the docks,
On the river the shadowy group, the big steam-tug closely flank'd on,
    each side by the barges, the hay-boat, the belated lighter,
On the neighboring shore the fires from the foundry chimneys burning
    high and glaringly into the night,
Casting their flicker of black contrasted with wild red and yellow light
    over the tops of houses, and down into the clefts of streets.

4

These and all else were to me the same as they are to you,
I loved well those cities, loved well the stately and rapid river,
The men and women I saw were all near to me,
Others the same—others who look back on me because I look'd forward
    to them,
(The time will come, though I stop here to-day and to-night.)

5

What is it then between us?
What is the count of the scores or hundreds of years between us?

Whatever it is, it avails not—distance avails not, and place avails not,
I too lived, Brooklyn of ample hills was mine,
I too walk'd the streets of Manhattan island, and bathed in the waters
    around it,
I too felt the curious abrupt questionings stir within me,
In the day among crowds of people sometimes they came upon me,
In my walks home late at night or as I lay in my bed they came upon me,
I too had been struck from the float forever held in solution,
I too had receiv'd identity by my body,
That I was I knew was of my body, and what I should be I knew I
    should be of my body.

6

It is not upon you alone that patches fall,
The dark threw its patches down upon me also
The best I had done seem'd to me blank and suspicious,
My great thoughts as I supposed them, were they not in reality meagre?
Nor is it you alone who know what it is to be evil,
I am he who knew what it was to be evil,
I too knitted the old knot of contrariety,
Blabb'd, blush'd, resented, lied, stole, grudg'd,
Had guile, anger, lust, hot wishes I dared not speak,
Was wayward, vain, greedy, shallow, sly, cowardly, malignant,
The wolf, the snake, the hog, not wanting in me,
The cheating look, the frivolous word, the adulterous wish, not wanting,
Refusals, hates, postponements, meanness, laziness, none of these wanting,
Was one with the rest, the days and haps of the rest,
Was call'd by my nighest name by clear loud voices of young men as
    they saw me approaching or passing,
Felt their arms on my neck as I stood, or the negligent leaning of their
    flesh against me as I sat,
Saw many I loved in the street or ferry-boat or public assembly, yet
    never told them a word,
Lived the same life with the rest, the same old laughing,
    gnawing, sleeping,
Play'd the part that still looks back on the actor or actress,
The same old role, the role that is what we make it, as great as we like,
Or as small as we like, or both great and small.

7

Closer yet I approach you,
What thought you have of me now, I had as much of you—I laid in my
    stores in advance,
I consider'd long and seriously of you before you were born.
Who was to know what should come home to me?
Who knows but I am enjying this?
Who knows, for all the distance, but I am as good as looking at you
    now, for all you cannot see me?

8

Ah, what can ever be more stately and admirable to me than mast-
    hemm'd Manhattan?
River and sunset and scallop-edg'd waves of flood-tide?
The sea-gulls oscillating their bodies, the hay-boat in the twilight, and
    the belated lighter?
What gods can exceed these that clasp me by the hand, and with voices I
    love call me promptly and loudly by my nighest name as I approach?
What is more subtle than this which ties me to the woman or man that
    looks in my face?
Which fuses me into you now, and pours my meaning into you?

We understand then do we not?
What I promis'd without mentioning it, have you not accepted?
What the study could not teach—what the preaching could not
    accomplish is accomplish'd, is it not?

9

Flow on, river! flow with the flood-tide, and ebb with the ebb-tide!
Frolic on, crested and scallop-edg'd waves!
Gorgeous clouds of the sunset! drench with your splendor me, or the
    men and women generations after me!
Cross from shore to shore, countless crowds of passengers!
Stand up, tall masts of Mannahatta! stand up, beautiful hills of Brooklyn!
Throb, baffled and curious brain! throw out questions and answers!
Suspend here and everywhere, eternal float of solution!
Gaze, loving and thirsting eyes, in the house or street or public assembly!
Sound out, voices of young men! loudly and musically call me by my
    nighest name!
Live, old life! play the part that looks back on the actor or actress!
Play the old role, the role that is great or small according as one makes it!
Consider, you who peruse me, whether I may not in unknown ways be
    looking upon you;
Be firm, rail over the river, to support those who lean idly, yet haste with
    the hasting current;
Fly on, sea-birds! fly sideways, or wheel in large circles high in the air;

Receive the summer sky, you water, and faithfully hold it till all
    downcast eyes have time to take it from you!
Diverge, fine spokes of light, from the shape of my bead, or any one's
    head, in the sunlit water!
Come on, ships rom the lower bay! pass up or down, white-sail'd
    schooners, sloops, lighters!
Flaunt away, flags of all nations! be duly lower'd at Sunset!
Burn high your fires, foundry chimneys! cast black shadows at nightfall!
    cast red and yellow light over the tops of the houses!
Appearances, now or henceforth, indicate what you are,
You necessary film, continue to envelop the soul,
About my body for me, and your body for you, be hung our divinest
    aromas,
Thrive, cities—bring your freight, bring your shows, ample and
    sufficient rivers,
Expand, being than which none else is perhaps more spiritual,
Keep your places, objects than which none else is more
    lasting.

You have waited, you always wait, you dumb, beautiful ministers,
We receive you with free sense at last, and are insatiate henceforward,
Not you any more shall be able to foil us, or withhold yourself.from us,
We use you, and do not cast you aside—we plant you permanently
    within us,
We fathom you not—we love you—there is perfection in you also,
You furnish your parts toward eternity,
Great or small you furnish your parts toward the soul.

A Broadway Pageant

Over the Western sea hither from Niphon come,
Courteous, the swart-cheek'd two-sworded envoys,
Leaning hack in their open barouches, bare-headed, impassive,
Ride to-day through Manhattan.

Libertad! I do not know whether others behold what I behold,
In the procession along with the nobles of Niphon, the errand-bearers,
Bringing up the rear, hovering above, around, or in the ranks marching,
But I will sing you a song of what I behold Libertad.

When million-footed Manhattan unpent descends to her pavements,
When the thunder-cracking guns arouse me with the proud roar I love,
When the round-mouth'd guns out of the smoke and smell I love spit
    their salutes,
When the fire-flashing guns have fully alerted me, and heaven-clouds
    canopy my city with a delicate thin haze,
When gorgeous the countless straight Stems, the forests at the wharves,
    thicken with colors,
When every ship richly drest carries her flag at the peak,
When pennants trail and street-festoons hang from the windows,
When Broadway is entirely given up to foot-passengers and foot-
    standers, when the mass is densest,
When the facades of the houses are alive with people,when eyes gaze
    riveted tens of thousands at a time,
When the guests from the islands advance, when the pageant moves
    forward visible,
When the summons is made, when the answer that waited thousands of
    years answers,
I too arising, answering, descend to the pavements, merge with the
    crowd, and gaze with them.

2

Superb-faced Manhattan!
Comrade Americanos! to us, then at last the Orient comes.

To us, my city,
Where our tall-topt marble and iron beauties range on opposite sides, to
    walk in the space between,
To-day our Antipodes comes.

The Originatress comes,
The nest of languages, the bequeather of poems, the race of eld,
Florid with blood, pensive, rapt with musings, hot with passion,
Sultry with perfume, with ample and flowing garments,
With sunburnt visage, with intense soul and glittering eyes,
The race of Brahma comes.

See my cantabile! these and more are flashing to us from the procession,
As it moves changing, a kaleidoscope divine it moves changing before
    us.
For not the envoys nor the tann'd Japanee from his island only,
Lithe and silent the Hindoo appears, the Asiatic continent itself appears,
    the past, the dead,
The murky night-morning of wonder and fable inscrutable,
The envelop'd mysteries, the old and unknown hive-bees,
The north, the sweltering south, eastern Assyria, the Hebrews, the
    ancient of ancients,
Vast desolated cities, the gliding present, all of these and more are in the
    pageant procession.

Geography, the world, is in it,
The Great Sea, the brood of islands, Polynesia, the coast beyond,
The coast you henceforth are facing—you Libertad! from your Western
    golden shores,
The countries there with their populations, the millions en-masse are
    curiously here,
The swarming market-places, the temples with idols ranged along the
    sides or at the end, bonze, brahmin, and llama,
Mandarin, farmer, merchant, mechanic, and fisherman,
The singing-girl and the dancing-girl, the ecstatic persons, the secluded
    emperors,
Confucius himself, the great poets and heroes, the warriors, he castes, all,
Trooping up, crowding from all directions, from the Altay mountains,
From Thibet, from the four winding and far-flowing rivers of China,

From the southern peninsulas and the demi-continental islands, from
    Malaysia,
These and whatever belongs to them palpable show forth to me, and are
    seiz'd by me,
And I am seiz'd by them, and friendlily held by them,
Till as here them all I chant, Libertad! for themselves
    and for you.

For I too raising my voice join the ranks of this pageant,
I am the chanter, I chant aloud over the pageant,
I chant the world on my Western sea,
I chant copious the islands beyond, thick as stars in the sky,
I chant the new empire grander than any before, as in a vision it comes
    to me,
I chant America the mistress, I chant a greater supremacy,
I chant projected a thousand blooming cities yet in time on those groups
    of sea-islands,
My sail-ships and steam-ships threading the archipelagoes,
My stars and stripes fluttering in the wind,
Commerce opening, the sleep of ages having done its work, races
    reborn, refresh'd,
Lives, works resumed—the object I know not—but the old, the Asiatic
    renew'd as it must be,
Commencing from this day surrounded by the world.

3

And you Libertad of the world
You shall sit in the middle well-pois'd thousands and thousands of years,
As to-day from one side the nobles of Asia come to you,
As to-morrow from the other side the queen of England sends her
    eldest son to you.
The sign is reversing, the orb is enclosed,
The ring is circled, the journey is done,
The box-lid is but perceptibly open'd, nevertheless the perfume pours
    copiously out of the whole box.
Young Libertad with the venerable Asia, the all-mother,
Be considerate with her now and ever hot Libertad, for
    you are all,

Bend your proud neck to the long-off mother now sending messages
    over the archipelagoes to you,
Bend your proud neck low for once, young Libertad.

Were the children straying westward so long? so wide the tramping?
Were the precedent dim ages debouching westward from Paradise so long?
Were the centuries steadily footing it that way, all the while unknown,
    for you, for reasons?

They are justified they are accomplish'd, they shall now be turn'd the
    other way also, to travel toward you thence,
They shall now also march obediently eastward for your sake Libertad.

Give Me The Splendid Silent Sun

Give me the splendid silent sun with all his beams full-dazzling,
Give me juicy autumnal fruit ripe and red from the orchard,
Give me a field where the unmow'd grass grows,
Give me an arbor, give me the trellis'd grape,
Give me fresh corn and wheat, give me serene-moving animals teaching
    content,
Give me nights perfectly quiet as on high plateaus west of the
    Mississippi, and I looking up at the stars,
Give me odorous at sunrise a garden of beautiful flowers where I can
    walk undisturb'd,
Give me for marriage a sweet-breath'd woman of whom I should never tire,
Give me a perfect child, give me away aside from the noise of the world
    a rural domestic life,
Give me to warble spontaneous songs recluse by myself, for my own
    ears only,
Give me solitude, give me Nature, give me again O Nature your primal
    sanities!

These demanding to have them, (tired with ceaseless excitement, and
    rack'd by the war-strife)
These to procure incessantly asking, rising in cries from my heart,
While yet incessantly asking still I adhere to my city,
Day upon day and year upon year O city, walking your streets,
Where you hold me enchain'd acertain time refusing to give me up,
Yet giving to make me glutted, enrich'd of soul, you give me forever faces;
(O I see what I sought to escape, confronting, reversing my cries,
I see my own soul trampling down what it ask'd for.)

2

Keep your splendid silent sun,
Keep your woods O Nature, and the quiet places by the woods,
Keep your fields of clover and timothy, and your corn-fields and orchards,
Keep the blossoming buckwheat fields where the Ninth-month bees hum;
Give me faces and streets—give me these phantoms incessant and
    endless along the trottoirs!

Give me interminable eyes—give me women—give me comrades and
    lovers by the thousand!
Let me see new ones every day—let me hold new ones by the hand
    every day!
Give me such shows—give me the Streets of Manhattan!
Give me Broadway, with the soldiers marching—give me the sound of
    the trumpets and drums!
(The soldiers in companies or regiments—some starting away, flush'd and
    reckless,
Some, their time up, returning with thinn'd ranks, young, yet very old,
    worn, marching, noticing nothing;)
Give me the shores and wharves heavy-fringed with black ships!
O such for me! O an intense life, full to repletion and varied!

The life of the theatre, bar-room, huge hotel, for me!
The saloon of the steamer! the crowded excursion for me! the torchlight
    procession!
The dense brigade bound for the war, with high piled military wagons
    following;
People, endless, streaming, with strong voices, passions, pageants,
Manhattan streets with their powerful throbs, with heating drums as now,
The endless and noisy chorus, the rustle and clank of muskets, (even the
    sight of the wounded)
Manhattan crowds, with their turbulent musical chorus!
Manhattan faces and eyes forever for me.

Proud Music of the Storm

Proud music of the storm,
Blast that careers so free, whistling across the prairies,
Strong hum of forest tree-tops—wind of the mountains,
Personified dim shapes—you hidden orchestras,
You serenades of phantoms with instruments alert,
Blending with Nature's rhythmus all the tongues of nations;
You chords left as by vast composers—you choruses,
You formless, free, religious dances—you from the Orient,
You undertone of rivers, roar of pouring cataracts,
You sounds from distant guns with galloping cavalry,
Echoes of camps with all the different bugle-calls,
Trooping tumultuous, filling the midnight late, bending me powerless,
Entering my lonesome slumber-chamber, why have you seiz'd me?

2

Come forward O my soul, and let the rest retire,
Listen, lose not, it is toward thee they tend,
Parting the midnight, entering my slumber-chamber,
For thee they sing and dance O soul.
A festival song,
The duet of the bridegroom and the bride, a marriage march,
With lips of love, and hearts of lovers fill'd to the brim with love,
The red-fiush'd cheeks and perfumes, the cortege swarming full of
    friendly faces young and old,
To flutes' clear notes and sounding harps' cantabile.
Now loud approaching drums,
Victoria! see'st thou in powder-smoke the banners torn but flying? the
    rout of the baffled?
Hearest those shouts of a conquering army?

(Ah soul, the sobs of women, the wounded groaning in agony,
The hiss and crackle of flames, the blacken'd ruins, the embers of cities,
The dirge and desolation of mankind.)

Now airs antique and medieval fill me,

I see and hear old harpers with their warps at Welsh festivals,
I hear the minnesingers singing their lays of love,
I hear the minstrels, gleemen, troubadburs, of the middle ages.

Now the great organ sounds,
Tremulous, while underneath, (as the hid footholds of the earth,
On which arising rest, and leaping forth depend,
All shapes of beauty, grace and strength, all hues we know,
Green blades of grass and warbling birds, children that gambol and play,
    the clouds of heaven above)
The strong base stands, and its pulsations intermits not,
Bathing, supporting, merging all the rest, maternity of all the rest,
And with it every instrument in multitudes,
The players playing, all the world's musicians,
The solemn hymns and masses rousing adoration,
All passionate heart-chants, sorrowful appeals,
The measureless sweet vocalists of ages,
And for their solvent setting earth's own diapason,
Of winds and woods and mighty ocean waves,
A new composite orchestra, binder of years and climes, tenfold renewer,
As of the far-back days the poets tell, the Paradiso,
The straying thence, the separation long, but now the wandering done,
The journey done, the journeyman come home,
And man and art with Nature fused again.

Tutti! for earth and heaven;
(The Almighty leader now for once has signal'd with his wand.)

The manly strophe of the husbands of the world,
And all the wives responding.

The tongues of violins,
(I think O tongues ye tell this heart, that cannot tell itself,
This brooding, yearning heart, that cannot tell itself.)

3

Ah from a little child,
Thou knowest soul how to me all sounds became music,

My mother's voice in lullaby or hymn,
(The voice,O tender voices, memory's loving voices,
Last miracle of all, O dearest mother's, Sister's, voices;)
The rain, the growing corn, the breeze among the long leav'd corn,
The measur'd sea-surf beating on the sand,
The twittering bird, the hawk's sharp scream,
The wild-fowl's notes at night as flying low migrating north
　　　or south,
The psalm in the country church or mid he clustering trees, the open air
　　　camp-meeting,
The fiddler in the tavern, the glee, the long-strung sailor song,
The lowing cattle, bleating sheep, the crowing cock at dawn.

All songs of current lands come sounding round me,
The German airs of friendship, wine and love,
, Irish ballads, merry jigs and dances, English warbles,
Chansons of France, Scotch tunes, and o'er the rest,
Italia'a peerless compositions.

Across the stage with pallor on her face, yet lurid passion,
Stalks Norma brandishing the dagger in her hand.

I see poor crazed Lucia's eyes' unnatural gleam,
Her hair down her back falls loose and dishevel'd.

I see where Ernani walking the bridal garden,
Amid the scent of night-roses, radiant, holding his bride by the hand,
Hears the infernal call, the death-pledge of the horn.

To crossing swords and gray hairs bared to heaven,
The clear electric base and baritone of the world,
The trombone duo, Libertad forever!

From Spanish chestnut trees' dense shade,
By old and heavy convent walls a wailing song.
Song of lost love, the torch of youth and life quench'd in despair,
Song of the dying swan, Fernando's heart is breaking.
Awaking from her woes at last retriev d Amina sings
Copious as stars and glad as morning light the torrents of her joy.

(The teeming lady comes,
The lustrious orb, Venus contralto, the blooming mother,
Sister of loftiest gods, Alboni's self I hear.)

4

I hear those odes, symphonies, operas,
I hear in the *William Tell* the music of an arous'd and angry people,
I hear Meyerbeer's *Huguenots*, the *Prophet*, or *Robert*,

Gounod's *Faust*, or Mozart's *Don Juan*.

I hear the dance-music of all nations,
The waltz, some delicious measure, lapsing, bathing me in bliss,
The bolero to tinkling guitars and clattering castanets.

I see religious dances old and new,
I hear the sound of the Hebrew lyre,
I see the crusaders marching bearing the cross on high, to the martial
    clang of cymbals;
I hear dervishes monotonously chanting, interspers'd with frantic
    shouts, as they spin around turning always towards Mecca,
I see the rapt religious dances of the Persians and the Arabs,
Again, at Eleusis, home of Ceres,
I see the modern Greeks
    dancing,
I hear them clapping their hands as they bend their bodies,
I hear the metrical shuffling of their feet.
I see again the wild old Corybantian dance, the performers wounding
    each other,
I see the Roman youth to the shrill sound of flageolets throwing and
    catching their weapons,
As they fall on their knees and rise again.

I hear from the Mussulman mosque the muezzin calling, I see the wor-
    shippers within, nor form nor sermon, argument nor word,
But silent, strange, devout, rais'd, glowing heads, ecstatic faces.
I hear the Egyptian harp of many strings,
The primitive chants of the Nile boatmen,

The sacred, imperial hymns of China,
To the delicate sounds of the king, (the stricken wood and stone)
Or to Hindu flutes and the fretting twang of the vina,
A band of bayaderes.

5

Now Asia, Africa leave me, Europe seizing inflates me,
To organs huge and bands I hear as from vast concourses of voices,
Luther's strong hymn *Eine feste Burg ist unser Gott*, Rossini's *Stabat Mater dolorosa*,
Or floating in some high cathedral dim with gorgeous color'd windows,
The passionate *Agnus Dei* or *Gloria in Excelsis*.

Composers mighty maestros
And you, sweet singers of old lands, soprani, tenor, bassi
To you a new bard caroling in the West,
Obeisant sends his love.
Such led to thee O soul,
All senses, shows and objects, lead to thee,
But now it seems to me sound leads o'er all the rest.)

I hear the annual singing of the children in St. Paul's cathedral,
Or, under the high roof of some colossal hail, the symphonies, oratorios
    of Beethoven, Handel, or Haydn,
The *Creation* in billows of Godhood laves me.

Give me to hold all sounds, (I madly struggling cry)
Fill me with all the voices of the universe,
Endow me with their throbbings, Nature's also,
The tempests, waters, winds, operas and chants, marches and dances,
Utter, pour in, for I would take them all!

6

Then I woke softly,
And pausing, questioning awhile the music of my dream,
And questioning all those reminiscences, the tempest in its fury,

And all the songs of sopranos and tenors.
And those rapt oriental dances of religious fervor,
And the sweet varied instruments, and the diapason of organs,
And all the artless plaints of love and grief and death,
I said to my silent curious soul out of the bed of the slumber-chamber,
Come, for I have found the clew I sought so long,
Let us go forth refresh'd amid the day,
Cheerfully tallying life, walking the world, the real,
Nourish'd henceforth by our celestial dream.
And I said, moreover,
Haply what thou hast heard O soul was not the sound of winds,
Nor dream of raging storm, nor sea-hawk's flapping wings nor harsh
    scream,
Nor vocalism of sun-bright Italy,
Nor German organ majestic, nor vast concourse of voices nor layers of
    harmonies,
Nor strophes of husbands and wives, nor sound of marching soldiers,
Nor flutes, nor harps, nor the bugle-calls of camps,
But to a new rhythmus fitted for thee,
Poems bridging the way from Life to Death, vaguely
    wafted in night air, uncaught, unwritten,
Which let us go forth in the bold day and write.

The Ox Tamer

In a far-away northern county in the placid pastoral region;
Lives my farmer friend, the theme of my recitative, a
    famous tamer of oxen,
There they bring him the three-year-olds and the four-year-olds to
    break them,
He will take the wildest Steer in the world and break him and tame him,
He will go fearless without any whip where the young bullock chafes up
    and down the yard,
The bullock's head tosses restless high in the air with raging eyes,
Yet see you! how soon his rage subsides—how soon this tamer tames
    him;
See you! on the farms hereabout a hundred oxen young and old, and he
    is the man who has tamed them,
They all know him, all are affectionate to him;
See you! some are such beautiful animals, so lofty looking;
Some are buff-color'd, some mottled, one has a white line running along
    his back, some are brindled,
Some have wide flaring horns (a good sign)—see you the bright hides,
See, the two with stars on their foreheads—see, the round bodies and
    broad backs,
How straight and square they stand on their legs—what fine sagacious
    eyes!
How they watch their tamer—they wish him near them—how they turn
    to look after him!
What yearning expression! how uneasy they are when he moves away
    from them;
Now I marvel what it can be he appears to them, (books, politics,
    poems, depart—all else departs)
I confess I envy only his fascination—my silent, illiterate friend,
Whom a hundred oxen love there in his life on farms,
In the northern county far, in the placid pastoral region.

After An Interval

(Nov. 22, 5875, Midnight—Saturn and Mars in conjunction)

After an interval, reading, here in the midnight,
With the great Stars looking on—all the stars of Orion looking,
And the silent Pleiades—and the duo looking of Saturn and ruddy Mars;
Pondering, reading my own songs, after a long interval,
    (sorrow and death familiar now)
Ere closing the book, what pride! what joy! to find them,
Standing so well the test of death and night!

And the duo of Saturn and Mars!

So Long!

Camerado, this is no book,
Who touches this touches a man,
(Is it night? are we here together alone ?)
It is I you hold and who holds you,
I spring from the pages into your arms—decease calls me forth.
O how your fingers drowse me,
Your breath falls around me like dew, your pulse lulls the
    tympans of my ears,
I feel immerged from head to foot,
Delicious, enough.

Enough O deed impromptu and secret,
Enough O gliding present—enough O summ'd-up past.

Dear friend whoever you are take this kiss,
I give it especially to you, do not forget me,
I feel like one who has done work for the day to retire awhile,
I receive now again of my many translations, from my avataras
    ascending, while others doubtless await me,
An unknown sphere more real than I dream'd, more direct, darts
    awakening rays about me, So long!
Remember my words, I may again return,
I love you, I depart from materials,
I am as one disembodied, triumphant, dead.

O Vast Rondure

O vast Rondure, swimming in space,
Cover'd all over with visible power and beauty,
Alternate light and day and the teeming spiritual darkness,
Unspeakable high processions of sun and moon and countless
    stars above,
Below, the manifold grass and waters, animals, mountains, trees,
With inscrutable purpose, some hidden prophetic intention,
Now first it seems my thought begins to span thee.

Down from the gardens of Asia descending radiating,
Adam and Eve appear, then their myriad progeny after them,
Wandering, yearning, curious, with restless explorations,
With questionings, baffled, formless, feverish, with never-happy hearts,
With that sad incessant refrain, *Wherefore unsatisfied soul?* and *Whither
    O mocking life?*

Ah who shall soothe these feverish children?
Who justify these restless explorations?
Who speak the secret of impassive earth?
Who bind it to us? what is this separate Nature so unnatural?
What is this earth to our affections? (unloving earth, without a throb to
    answer ours,
Cold earth, the place of graves)
Yet soul be sure the first intent remaips, and shall be carried out,
Perhaps even now the time has arrived.

After the seas are all cross'd, (as they seem already cross'd)
After the great captains and engineers have accomplish'd their work,
After the noble inventors, after the scientists, the chemist, the geologist,
    ethnologist,
Finally shall come the poet worthy that name,
The true son of God shall come singing his songs.

The Red Squaw

Now what my mother told me one day as we sat at dinner together,
Of when she was a nearly grown girl living home with her parents on
   the old homestead.

A red squaw came one breakfast-time to the old homestead,
On her back she carried a bundle of rushes for rush-bottoming chairs,
Her hair, straight, shiny, coarse, black, profuse, half-envelop'd her face,
Her step was free and elastic, and her voice sounded exquisitely as
     she spoke.

My mother look'd in delight and amazement at the stranger,
She look'd at the freshness of her tall-borne face and full
     and pliant limbs,
The more she look'd upon her she loved her,
Never before had she seen such wonderful beauty and purity,
She made her sit on a bench by the jamb of the fireplace,
   she cook'd food for her,
She had no work to give her, but she gave her remembrance and fondness.

The red squaw staid all the forenoon, and toward the middle of the
     afternoon she went away,
O my mother was loth to have her go away,
All the week she thought of her, she watch'd for her many a month,
She remember'd her many a winter and many a summer,
But the red squaw never came nor was heard of there
     again.

An Old Stage-Driver

A reminiscence of the vulgar fate,
A frequent sample of the life and death of workmen,
Each after his kind.

Cold dash of waves at the ferry-wharf, posh and ice in the river, half-
   frozen mud in the streets,
A gray discouraged sky overhead, the short last daylight of December,
A hearse and stages, the funeral of an old Broadway stage-driver, the
   cortege mostly drivers.

Steady the trot to the cemetery, duly rattles the death-bell,
The gate is pass'd, the new-dug grave is halted at, the living alight,
   the hearse uncloses,
The coffin is pass'd out, lower'd and settled, the whip is laid on the
   coffin, the earth is swiftly shovel'd in,
The mound above is flatted with the spades—silence,
A minute—no one moves or speaks—it is done,
He is decently put away—is there any thing more?

He was a good fellow, free-mouth'd, quick-temper'd, not bad-looking,
Ready with life or death for a friend, fond of women, gambled, ate
   hearty, drank hearty,
Had known what it was to be flush, grew low-spirited toward the last,
   sicken'd, was help'd by a contribution,
Died, aged forty-one years—and that was his funeral.

Thumb extended, finger uplifted, apron, cape, gloves, strap, wet-weather
   clothes, whip carefully chosen,
Boss, spotter, starter, hostler, somebody loafing on you, you loafing on
   somebody, headway, man before and man behind,
Good day's work, bad day's work, pet stock, mean stock, first out, last
   out, turning-in at night,
To think that these are so much and so nigh to other drivers, and he
   there takes no interest in them.

Inscriptions

One's Self I Sing

One's Self I sing, simple separate person,
Yet utter the word Democratic, the word En-masse.

Of physiology from top to toe I sing,
Not physiognomy alone nor brain alone is worthy for the
Muse, I say the Form complete is worthier far,
The Female equally with the Male I sing.

Of Life immense in passion, pulse, and power,
Cheerful, for freest action form'd under the laws divine,
The Modern man I sing.

To Foreign Lands

I heard that you ask'd for something to prove this puzzle the New World,
And to define America, her athletic Democracy,
Therefore I send you my poems that you behold in them what you wanted.

I Hear America Singing

I Hear America singing, the varied carols I hear,
Those of mechanics, each one singing his as it should be.
    blithe and strong,
The carpenter singing his as he measures his plank or beam,
The mason singing his as he makes ready for work, or leaves off work,
The boatman singing what belongs to him in his boat, the deckhand
    singing on the steamboat deck,
The shoemaker singing as he sits on his bench, the hatter singing as
    he stands,
The wood-cutter's song, the plaughboy's on his way in the morning, or
    at noon intermission or at sundown,
The delicious singing of the mother, or of the young wife at work, or of
    the girl sewing or washing,
Each singing what belongs to him or her and to none else,
The day what belongs to the day—at night the party of young fellows,
    robust, friendly,
Singing with open mouths their strong melodious songs.

Shut Not Your Doors

Shut not your doors to me proud libraries,
For that which was lacking on all your well-fill'd shelves,
  yet needed most, I bring,
Forth from the war emerging, a book I have made,
The words of my book nothing, the drift of it every thing.
A book separate, not link'd with the rest nor felt by the intellect,
But you ye untold latencies will thrill to every page.

Calamus

Whoever you are Holding Me Now in Hand

Whoever you are holding me now in hand,
Without one thing all will be useless,
I give you fair warning before you attempt me further,
I am not what you supposed, but far different.

Who is he that would become my follower?
Who would sign himself a candidate for my affections?

The way is suspicious, the result uncertain, perhaps destructive,
You would have to give up all else, I alone would expect to be your sole
    and exclusive standard,
Your novitiate would even then be long and exhausting,
The whole past theory of your life and all conformity to the lives around
    you would have to be abandon'd,
Therefore release me now before troubling yourself any further, let go
    your hand from my shoulders,
Put me down and depart on your way.

Or else by stealth in some wood for trial,
Or back of a rock in the open air,
(For in any roof'd room of a house I emerge not, nor in company,
And in libraries I lie as one dumb, a gawk, or unborn, or dead)
But just possibly with you on a high hill, first watching lest any person for
    miles around approach unawares,
Or possibly with you sailing at sea, or on the beach of the sea or some
    quiet island,
Here to put your lips upon mine I permit you,

With the comrade's long-dwelling kiss or the new husband's kiss,
For I am the new husband and I am the comrade.

Or if you will, thrusting me beneath your clothing,
Where I may feel the throbs of your heart or rest upon your hip,
Carry me when you go forth over land or sea;
For thus merely touching you is enough, is best,
And thus touching you would I silently sleep and be carried eternally.

But these leaves conning you con at peril,
For these leaves and me you will not understand,
They will elude you at first and still more afterward, I will certainly
    elude you,
Even while you should think you had unquestionably caught me, behold!
Already you see I have escaped from you.

For it is not for what I have put into it that I have written this book,
Nor is it by reading it you will acquire it,
Nor do those know me best who admire me and vauntingly
praise me,
Nor will the candidates for my love (unless at most a very few) prove
    victorious,
Nor will my poems do good only, they will do just as much evil,
    perhaps more,
For all is useless without that which you may guess at many times and
    not hit, that which I hinted at;
Therefore release me and depart on your way.

The Base of All Metaphysics

And now gentlemen,
A word I give to remain in your memories and minds,
As base and finale` too for all metaphysics.

(So to the students the old professor,
At the close of his crowded course.)

Having studied the new and antique, the Greek and Germanic systems,
Kant having studied and stated, Fichte and Schelling and Hegel,
Stated the lore of Plato, and Socrates greater than Plato,
And greater than Socrates sought and stated, Christ divine having
    studied long,
I see reminiscent to-day those Greek and Germanic systems,
See the philosophies all, Christian churches and tenets see,
Yet underneath Socrates clearly see, and underneath Christ
    the divine I see,
The dear love of mao for his comrade, the attraction of friend to friend,
Of the well-married husband and wife, of children and parents,
Of city for city and land for land.

When I Heard at the Close of Day

When I heard at the close of the day how my name had been receiv'd
    with plaudits in the capitol, still it was not a happy night for me that
    follow'd,
And else when I carous'd, or when my plans were accomplished, still I
    was not happy,
But the day when I rose at dawn from the bed of perfect health,
    refresh'd, singing, inhaling the ripe breath of autumn,
When I saw the full moon in the west grow pale and disappear in the
    morning light,
When I wander'd alone over the beach, and undressing bathed, laughing
    with the cool waters, and saw the sun rise,
And when I thought how my dear friend my lover was on his way coming,
    O then I was happy,
O then each breath tasted sweeter, and all that day my food nourish'd
    me more, and the beautiful day pass'd well,
And the next came with equal joy, and with the next at evening came
    my friend,
And that night while all was still I heard the waters roll slowly
    continually up the shores,
I heard the hissing rustle of the liquid and sands as directed to me whis-
    pering to congratulate me,
For the one I love most lay sleeping by me under the same cover in the
    cool night,
In the stillness in the autumn moonbeams his face was inclined toward me,
And his arm lay lightly around my breast—and that night I was happy.

Children of Adam

❧❦

I Sing the Body Electric

1

I sing the body electric,
The armies of those I love engirth me and I engirth them,
They will not let me off till I go with them, respond to them,
And discorrupt them, and charge them full with the charge of the soul.

Was it doubted that those who corrupt their own bodies conceal
    themselves?
And if those who defile the living are as bad as they who defile the dead?
And if the body does not do fully as much as the Soul? And if the body
were not the Soul, what is the Soul?

2

The love of the Body of man or woman balks account, the body itself
    balks account,
That of the male is perfect, and that of the female is perfect.

The expression of the face balks account,
But the expression of a well-made man appears not only in his face,
It is in his limbs and joints also, it is curiously in the joints of his hips
    and wrists,

It is in his walk, the carriage of his neck, the flex of his waist and knees,
    dress does not hide him,
The strong sweet quality he has strikes through the cotton and broad-
    cloth,
To see him pass conveys as much as the best poem, perhaps more,
You linger to see his back, and the back of his neck and shoulder-side.

The sprawl and fullness of babes, the bosoms and heads of women, the
    folds of their dress, their style as we pass in the street, the contour
    of their shape downwards,
The swimmer naked in the swimming-bath, seen as he swims through
    the transparent green-shine, or lies with his face up and rolls silently
    to and from the heave of the water,
The bending forward and backward of rowers in row-boats, the horse-
    man in his saddle,
Girls, mothers, house-keepers, in all their performances,
The group of laborers seated at noon-time with their open dinner-ket-
    tles, and their wives waiting,
The female soothing a child, the farmer's daughter in the garden of cow-
    yard,
The young fellow hosing corn, the sleigh-driver driving his six horses
    through the crowd,
The wrestle of wrestlers, two apprentice-boys, quite grown, lusty, good-
    natured, native-born, out on the vacant lot at sundown after work,
The coats and caps thrown down, the embrace of love and resistance,
The upper-hold and under-hold, the hair rumpled over and blinding the
    eyes;
The march of firemen in their own costumes, the play of masculine
    muscle through clean-setting trowsers and waist-straps,
The slow return from the fire, the pause when the bell strikes suddenly
    again, and the listening on the alert,
The natural, perfect, varied attitudes, the bent head, the curv'd neck and
    the counting;
Such-like I love—I loosen myself, pass freely, am at the mother's breast
    with the little child,
Swim with the swimmers, wrestle with wrestlers, march in line with the
    firemen, and pause, listen, count.

3

I knew a man, a common farmer—the father of five sons,
And in them the fathers of sons—and in them the fathers of sons.

This man was a wonderful vigor, calmness, beauty of person,
The shape of his head, the pale yellow and white of his hair and beard,
    the immeasurable meaning of his black eyes, the richness and
    breadth of his manners,
These I used to go and visit him to see, he was wise also,
He was six feet tall, he was over eighty years old—his sons were
    massive, clean, bearded, tan-faced, handsome,
They and his daughters loved him—all who saw him loved him,
They did not love him by allowance—they loved him with personal
    love;
He drank water only—the blood show'd like scarlet through the clear-
    brown skin of his face;
He was a frequent gunner and fisher—he sail'd his boat himself, he had a
    fine one presented to him by a ship-joiner—he had fowling-pieces
    presented to him by men that loved him;
When he went with his five sons and many grand-sons to hunt or fish,
    you would pick him out as the most beautiful and vigorous of
    the gang.
You would wish long and long to be with him—you would wish to sit
    by him in the boat that you and he might touch each other.

4

I have perceiv'd that to be with those I like is enough,
To stop in company with the rest at evening is enough,
To be surrounded by beautiful, curious, breathing, laughing flesh is
    enough,
To pass among them or touch any one, or rest my arm ever so lightly
    round his or her neck for a moment, what is this then?
I do not ask any more delight—I swim in it, as in a sea.

There is something in staying close to men and women and looking on
    them, and in the contact and odor of them, that pleases the soul well,
All things please the soul, but these please the soul well.

5

This is the female form;
A divine nimbus exhales from it from head to foot;
It attracts with fierce undeniable attraction!
I am drawn by its breath as if I were no more than a helpless vapor, all
    falls aside but myself and it;
Books, art, religion, time, the visible and solid earth, and what was
    expected of heaven or fear'd of hell, are now consumed;
Mad filaments, ungovernable shoots play out of it, the response likewise
    ungovernable;
Hair, bosom, hips, bend of legs, negligent falling hands all diffused,
    mine too diffused;
Ebb stung by the flow and flow stung by the ebb, love-flesh swelling
    and deliciously aching;
Limitless limpid jets of love hot and enormous, quivering jelly of love,
    white-blow and delirious juice;
Bridegroom night of love working surely and softly into the
    prostrate dawn,
Undulating into the willing and yielding day,
Lost in the cleave of the clasping and sweet-flesh'd day.
This the nucleus—after the child is born of woman, man is born
    of woman;
This the bath of birth, this the merge of small and large, and the
    outlet again.

Be not ashamed women, your privilege encloses the rest, and is the exit
    of the rest;
You are the gates of the body, and you are the gates of the soul.

The female contains all qualities and tempers them—
    she is in her place and moves with perfect balance,
She is all things duly veil'd, she is both passive and active,
She is to conceive daughters as well as sons, and sons as well as daughters.

As I see my soul reflected in Nature,
As I see through a mist, One with inexpressible completeness,
    sanity, beauty,
See the bent head and arms folded over the breast—the female I see.

6

The male is not less the soul nor more, he too is in his place,
He too is all qualities, he is action and power,
The flush of the known universe is in him,
Scorn becomes him well, and appetite and defiance become him well,
The wildest largest passions, bliss that is utmost, sorrow that is utmost
    become him well, pride is for him,
The full-spread pride of man is calming and excellent to the soul,
Knowledge becomes him, he likes it always, he brings every thing to the
    test of himself,
Whatever the survey, whatever the sea and the sail he strikes soundings
    at last only here,
(Where else does he strike soundings except here?)

The man's body is sacred and the woman's body is sacred,
No matter who it is, it is sacred—is it the meanest one in the
    laborers' gang?
Is it one of the dull-faced immigrants just landed on the wharf?
Each belongs here or anywhere just as much as the well-off, just as
    much as you,
Each has his or her place in the procession.
(All is a procession,
The universe is a procession with measured and perfect motion.)

Do you know so much yourself that you call the meanest ignorant?
Do you suppose you have a right to a good sight, and he or she has no
    right to a sight?
Do you think matter has cohered together from its diffuse float, and the
    soil is on the surface, and water runs and vegetation sprouts,
For you only, and not for him and her?

7

A man's body at auction
(For before the war I often go to the slave-mart and watch the sale),
I help the auctioneer, the sloven does not half know his business.

Gentlemen look on this wonder,

Whatever the bids of the bidders they cannot be high enough for it,
For it the globe lay preparing quintillions of years without one animal
    or plant,
For it the revolving cycles truly and steadily roll'd.

In this head the all-baffling brain,
In it and below it the makings of heroes.

Examine these limbs, red, black, or white, they are cunning in tendon
    and nerve,
They shall be stript that you may see them.
Exquisite senses, life-lit eyes, pluck, volition,
Flakes of breast-muscle, pliant backbone and neck, flesh not flabby,
    good-sized arms and legs,
And wonders within there yet.

Within there runs blood,
The same old blood! the same red-running blood!
There swells and jets a heart, there all passions, desires, reachings,
    aspirations,
(Do you think they are not there because they are not express'd in parlors
    and lecture-rooms?)

This is not only one man, this the father of those who shall be fathers in
    their turns,
In him the start of populous states and rich republics,
Of him countless immortal lives with countless embodiments and
    enjoyments.

How do you know who shall come from the offspring of his offspring
    through the centuries?
(Who might you find you have come from yourself, if you could trace
    back through the centuries?)

8

A woman's body at auction,
She too is not only herself, she is the teeming mother of mothers,
She is the bearer of them that shall grow and be mates to the mothers.

Have you ever loved the body of a woman?
Have you ever loved the body of a man?
Do you not see that these are exactly the same to all in all nations and
    times all over the earth?

If any thing is sacred the human body is sacred,
And the glory and sweet of a man is the token of manhood untainted,
And in man or woman a clean, strong, firm-fibred body, is more
    beautiful than the most beautiful face.
Have you seen the fool that corrupted his own live body? or the fool
    that corrupted her own live body?
For they do not conceal themselves, and cannot conceal themselves.

9

O my body! I dare not desert the likes of you in other men and women,
    nor the likes of the parts of you,
I believe the likes of you are to stand or fall with the likes of the soul,
    (and that they are the soul)
I believe the likes of you shall stand or fall with my poems, and that
    they are my poems,
Man's, woman's, child, youth's, wife's, husband's, mother's, father's, young
    man's, young woman's poems,
Head, neck, hair, ears, drop and tympan of the ears,
Eyes, eye-fringes, iris of the eye, eyebrows, and the waking or sleeping of
    the lids,
Mouth, tongue, lips, teeth, roof of the mouth, jaws, and the jaw-hinges,
Nose, nostrils of the nose, and the partition,
Cheeks, temples, forehead, chin, throat, back of the neck, neck-slue,
Strong shoulders, manly beard, scapula, hind-shoulders, and the ample
    side-round of the chest,
Upper-arm, armpit, elbow-socket, lower-arm, arm-sinews, arm-bones,
Wrist and wrist-joints, hand, palm, knuckles, thumb, forefinger, finger-
    joints, finger-nails,
Broad breast-front, curling hair of the breast, breast-bone, breast-side,
Ribs, belly, backbone, joints of the backbone,
Hips, hip-sockets, hip-strength, inward and outward round, man-balls,
    man-root,
Strong set of thighs, well carrying the trunk above,

Leg-fibres, knee, knee-pan, upper-leg, under-leg,
Ankles, instep, foot-ball, toes, toe-joints, the heel;
All attitudes, all the shapeliness, all the belongings of my or your body
    or of any one's body, male or female,
The lung-sponges, the stomach-sac, the bowels sweet and clean,
The brain in its folds inside the skull-frame,
Sympathies, heart-valves, palate-valves, sexuality, maternity,
Womanhood, and all that is a woman, and the man that comes from
    woman,
The womb, the teats, nipples, breast-milk, tears, laughter, weeping, love-
    looks, love-perturbations and risings,
The voice, articulation, language, whispering, shouting aloud,
Food, drink, pulse, digestion, sweat, sleep, walking, swimming,
Poise on the hips, leaping, reclining, embracing, arm-curving and tight-
    ening,
The continual changes of the flex of the mouth, and around the eyes,
The skin, the sunburnt shade, freckles, hair,
The curious sympathy one feels when feeling with the hand the naked
    meat of the body,
The circling rivers the breath, and breathing it in and out,
The beauty of the waist, and thence of the hips, and thence downward
    toward the knees,
The thin red jellies within you or within me, the bones and the marrow
    in the bones,
The exquisite realization of health;
O I say these are not the parts and poems of the body only, but of the
    soul,
O I say now these are the soul!

A Woman Waits For Me

A woman waits for me—she contains all, nothing is lacking,
Yet all were lacking, if sex were lacking, or if the moisture of
    the right man were lacking.

Sex contains all,
Bodies, Souls, meanings, proofs, purities, delicacies, results,
    promulgations,
Songs, commands, health, pride, the maternal mystery, the seminal milk;
All hopes, benefactions, bestowals,
All the passions, loves, beauties, delights of the earth,
All the governments, judges, gods, follow'd persons of the earth,
These are contain'd in sex, as parts of itself, and justifications of itself.

Without shame the man I like knows and avows the deliciousness of his
    sex,
Without shame the woman I like knows and avows hers.

Now I will dismiss myself from impassive women,
I will go stay with her who waits for me, and with those women that are
    warm-blooded and sufficient for me;
I see that they understand me, and do not deny me;
I see that they are worthy of me—I will be the robust husband of those
    women.

They are not one jot less than I am,
They are tann'd in the face by shining suns and blowing winds,
Their flesh has the old divine suppleness and strength,
They know how to swim, row, ride, wrestle, shoot, run, strike, retreat,
    advance, resist, defend themselves,
They are ultimate in their own right—they are calm, clear, well-
    possess'd of themselves.

I draw you close to me, you women!
I cannot let you go, I would do you good,
I am for you, and you are for me, not only for our own sake, but for
    others' sakes;

Envelop'd in you sleep greater heroes and bards,
They refuse to awake at the touch of any man but me,

It is I, you women—I make my way,
I am stern, acrid, large, undissuadable—but I love you,
I do not hurt you any more than is necessary for you,
I pour the stuff to start Sons and daughters fit for These States—I press
    with slow rude muscle,
I brace myself effectually—I listen to no entreaties,
I dare not withdraw till I deposit what has so long accumulated within me.

Through you I drain the pent-up rivers of myself,
In you I wrap a thousand onward years,.
On you I graft the grafts of the best-beloved of me and America,
The drops I distil upon you shall grow fierce and athletic girls, new
    artists, musicians, and singers,
The babes I beget upon you are to beget babes in their turn,
I shall demand perfect men and women out of my love-spendings,
I shall expect them to interpenetrate with others, as I and you
    interpenetrate now,
I shall count on the fruits of the gushing showers of them, as I count on
    the fruits of the gushing showers I give now,
I shall look for loving crops from the birth, life, death, immortality, I
    plant so lovingly now.

Spontaneous Me

The arm of roy friend hanging idly over my shoulder,
The hill-side whiten'd with blossoms of the mountain ash,
The same, late in autumn—the hues of red, yellow, drab, purple, and
    light and dark green,
The rich coverlid of the grass—animals and birds—the private untrim-
    m'd bank—the primitive apples—the pebble-stones,
Beautiful dripping fragments—the negligent list of one after another, as I
    happen to call them to me, or think of them,
The real poems, (what we call poems being merely pictures)
The poems of the privacy of the night, and of men like me,
This poem, drooping shy and unseen, that I always carry, and that all
    men carry,
(Know, once for all, avow'd on purpose, wherever are men like me, are
    our lusty, lurking, masculine poems;)
Love-thoughts, love-juice, love-odor, love-yielding, love-climbers, and
    the climbing sap,
Arms and hands of love—lips of love—phallic thumb of love— breasts
    of love—bellies press'd and glued together with love,
Earth of chaste love—life that is only life after love,
The body of my love—the body of the woman I love—the body of the
    man—the body of the earth,
Soft forenoon airs that blow from the south-west,
The hairy wild-bee that murmurs and hankers up and down-that gripes
    the full-grown lady-flower, curves upon her with amorous firm legs,
    takes his will of her, and holds himself tremulous and tight till he is
    satisfied,
The wet of woods through the early hours,
Two sleepers at night lying close together as they sleep, one with an arm
    slanting down across and below the waist of the other,
The smell of apples, aromas from crush'd sage-plant, mint, birch-bark,
The boy's longings, the glow and pressure as he confides to me what he
    was dreaming,
The dead leaf whirling its spiral whirl, and falling still and content to the
    ground,
The no-form'd stings that sights, people, objects, sting me with,
The hubb'd sting of myself, stinging me as much as it ever can any one,

The sensitive, orbic, underlapp'd brothers, that only privileged feelers
    may be intimate where they are,
The curious roamer, the hand, roaming all over the body—the bashful
    withdrawing of flesh where the fingers soothingly pause and edge
    themselves,
The limpid liquid within the young man,
The vexed corrosion, so pensive and so painful,
The torment—the irritable tide that will not be at rest,
The like of the same I feel—the like of the same in others,
The young man that flushes and flushes, and the young woman that
    flushes and flushes,
The young man that wakes, deep at night, the hot hand seeking to
    repress what would master him;
The mystic amorous night'—the strange half-welcome pangs, visions,
    sweats,
The pulse pounding through palms and trembling encircling fingers—the
    young man all color'd, red, ashamed, angry;
The souse upon me of my lover the sea, as I lie willing and naked,
The merriment of the twin-babes that crawl over the grass in the sun,
    the mother never turning her vigilant eyes from them,
The walnut-trunk, the walnut-husks, and the ripening or ripen'd long-
    round walnuts;
The continence of vegetables, birds, animals,
The consequent meanness of me should I skulk or find myself indecent,
    while birds and animals never once skulk or find themselves indecent;
The great chastity of paternity, to match the great chastity of maternity,
The oath of procreation I have sworn—my Adamic and fresh daughters,
The greed that eats me day and night with hungry gnaw, till I saturate
    what shall produce boys to fill my place when I am through,
The wholesome relief, repose, content;
And this bunch, pluck'd at random from myself;
It has done its work—I tossed it carelessly to fall where it may.

One Hour To Madness and Joy

One hour to madness and joy!
O furious! O confine me not!
(What is this that frees me so in storms?
What do my shouts amid lightnings and raging winds mean?)

O to drink the mystic deliria deeper than any other man!
O savage and tender achings!
(I bequeath them to you, my children,
I tell them to you, for reasons, O bridegroom and bride.)

O to be yielded to you, whoever you are, and you to be yielded to me,
    in defiance of the world!
O to return to Paradise! O bashful and feminine!
O to draw you to me—to plant on you for the first time the lips of a
    determin'd man!

O the puzzle—the thrice-tied knot—the deep and dark pool! O all
    untied and illumin'd!
O to speed where there is space enough and air enough at last!
O to be absolv'd from previous ties and conventions! from mine, and
    you from yours!
O to find a new unthought-of nonchalance with the best of nature!
O to have the gag remov'd from one's mouth!
O to have ëthe feeling, to-day or any day, I am sufficient as I am!

O something unprov'd! something in a trance!
O madness amorous! O trembling!
O to escape utterly from others' anchors and holds!
To drive free! to love free! to dash reckless and dangerous!
To court destruction with taunts—with invitations!
To ascend—to leap to the heavens of the love indicated to me!
To rise thither with my inebriate Soul!
To be lost, if it must be so
To feed the remainder of life with one hour of fullness and freedom!
With one brief hour of madness and joy.

I Heard You, Solemn, Sweet Pipes of the Organ

I heard you, solemn-sweet pipes of the organ, as last Sunday morn I
    pass'd the church;
Winds of autumn!—as I walk'd the woods at dusk, I heard your long-
    stretch'd sighs, up above, so mournful;
I heard the perfect Italian tenor, singing at the opera—I heard the sopra-
    no in the midst of the quartet singing;
Heart of my love!—you too I heard, murmuring low, through one of the
    wrists around my head;
Heard the pulse of you, when all was still, ringing little bells last night
    under my ear.

I Am He That Aches With Love

I am he that aches with amorous love;
Does the earth gravitate? Does not all matter, aching, attract
    all matter?
So the Body of me, to all I meet, or know.

We Two—How Long We Were Fool'd

We two—how long we were fool'd!
Now transmuted, we swiftly escape, as Nature escapes
We are Nature—long have we been absent, but now we return;
We become plants, leaves, foliage, roots, bark;
We are bedded in the ground—we are rocks;
We are oaks—we grow in the openings side by side;
We browse—we are two among the wild herds, spontaneous as any;
We are two fishes swimming in the sea together;
We are what the locust blossoms are—we drop scent around the lanes,
    mornings and evenings;
We are also the coarse smut of beasts, vegetables, minerals;
We are two predatory hawks—we soar above, and look down;
We are two resplendent suns—we it is who balance ourselves, orbic and
    stellar—we are as two comets;
We prowl fang'd and four-footed in the woods—we spring on prey;
We are two clouds, forenoons and afternoons, driving overhead;
We are seas mingling—we are two of those cheerful waves, rolling over
    each other, and interwetting each other;
We are what the atmosphere is, transparent, receptive, pervious,
    impervious:
We are snow, rain, cold, darkness—we are each product and influence
    of the globe;
We have circled and circled till we have arrived home again—
    we two have;
We have voided all but freedom, and all but our own joy.

Out of the Rolling Ocean, the Crowd

1

Out of the rolling ocean, the crowd, came a drop gently to me,
Whispering, *I love you, before long I die,*
I have travel'd a long way, merely to look on you, to touch you,
For I could not die till I once look'd on you,
For I fear'd I might afterward lose you.

2

(Now we have met, we have look'd, we are safe;
Return in peace to the ocean, my love;
I too am part of that ocean, my love—we are not so much separated;
Behold the great rondure—the cohesion of all, how perfect!
But as for me, for you, the irresistible sea is to separate us,
As for an hour, carrying us diverse—yet cannot carry us diverse for ever;
Be not impatient—a little space—Know you, I salute the air, the ocean
    and the land,
Every day, at sundown, for your dear sake, my love.)

Native Moments

Native moments! when you come upon me—Ah you are here now!
Give me now libidinous joys only!
Give me the drench of my passions! Give me life coarse and rank!
To-day, I go consort with nature's darlings-to-night too;
I am for those who believe in loose delights—I share the midnight orgies
    of young men;
I dance with the dancers and drink with the drinkers;
The echoes ring with our indecent calls;
I take for my love some prostitute—I pick out some low person for my
    dearest friend,
He shall be lawless, rude, illiterate—he shall be one condemn'd by others
    for deeds done;
I will play a part no longer—Why should I exile myself from my com-
    panions?
O you shunn'd persons! I at least do not shun you,
I come forthwith in your midst—I will be your poet,
I will be more to you than to any of the rest.

Once I Pass'd Through a Populous City

Once I pass'd through a populous city, imprinting my brain, for future
    use, with its shows, architecture, customs, and traditions;
Yet now, of all that city, I remember only a woman I casually met there,
    who detain'd me for love of me;
Day by day and night by night we were together—All else has long been
    forgotten by me;
I remember, I say, only that woman who passionately clung to me;
Again we wander—we love—we separate again;
Again she holds me by the hand—I must not go!
I see her close beside me, with silent lips, sad and tremulous.

Facing West From California's Shores

Facing west, from California's shores,
Inquiring, tireless, seeking what is yet unfound,
I, a child, very old, over waves, towards the house of maternity, the land
    of migrations, look afar,
Look off the shores of my Western Sea—the circle almost circled;
For, starting westward from Hindustan, from the vales of Kashmere,
From Asia-from the north—from the God, the sage, and the hero,
From the south—from the flowery peninsulas, and the spice islands,
Long having wander'd since—round the earth having wander'd,
Now I face home again—very pleas'd and joyous;
(But where is what I started for, so long ago?
And why is it yet unfound?)

Ages and Ages, Returning at Intervals

Ages and ages, returning at intervals,
Undestroy'd, wandering immortal,
Lusty, phallic, with the potent original loins, perfectly sweet,
I, chanter of Adamic songs,
Through the new garden, the West, the great cities calling,
Deliriate, thus prelude what is generated, offering these, offering myself,
Bathing myself, bathing my songs in Sex,
Offspring of my loins.

O Hymen! O Hymenee!

O Hymen! O hymenee!
Why do you tantalize me thus?
O why sting me for a swift moment only?
Why can you not continue? O why do you now cease?
Is it because, if you continued beyond the swift moment, you would soon
    certainly kill me?

As Adam, Early in the Morning

As Adam, early in the morning,
Walking forth from the bower, refresh'd with sleep;
Behold me where I pass—hear my voice—approach,
Touch me—touch the palm of your hand to my Body as I pass;
Be not afraid of my Body.

Drum-Taps

Ethiopia Saluting the Colors

Who are you dusky woman, so ancient hardly human, With your woolly-
    white and turband head, and bare bony feet?
Why rising by the roadside here, do you the colors greet?

('Tis while our army lines Carolina's sand and pines,
Forth from thy hovel door thou Ethiopia com'st to me,
As under doughty Sherman I march toward the sea.)

Me master years a hundred since from my parents sunder'd,
A little child, they caught me as the savage beast is caught,
Then hither me across the sea the cruel slaver brought.

No further does she say, but lingering all the day,
Her high-borne turban'd head she wags, and rolls her darkling eye,
And courtesies to the regiments, the guidons moving by.

What is it fateful woman, so blear, hardly human?
Why wag your head with turban bound, yellow, red and green?
Are the things so strange and marvelous you see or have seen?

To a Certain Civilian

Did you ask dulcet rhymes from me?
Did you seek the civilian's peaceful and languishing rhymes?
Did you find what I sang erewhile so hard to follow?
Why I was not singing erewhile for you to follow', to understand; nor
    am I now;
(I have been born of the same as the war was born,
The drum-corps' rattle is ever to me sweet music, I love well the martial
    dirge,
With slow wail and convulsive throb leading the officers funeral;)
What to such as you anyhow such a poet as I? therefore leave my works,
And go lull yourself with what you can understand, and with piano-tunes,
For I lull nobody, and you will never understand me.

Spirit Whose Work Is Never Done
(Washington City, 1865)

Spirit whose work is done—spirit of dreadful hours!
Ere departing fade from my eyes your forests of bayonets;
Spirit of gloomiest fears and doubts, (yet onward ever unfaltering
    pressing)
Spirit of many a solemn day and many a savage scene; electric spirit,
That with muttering voice through the war now closed, like a tireless
    phantom. flitted,
Rousing the land with breath of flame, while you beat and beat the drum,
Now as the sound of the drum, hollow and harsh to the last,
    reverberates round me,
As your ranks, your immortal ranks, return, return from the battles,
As the muskets of the young men yet lean over their shoulders,
As I look on the bayonets bristling over their shoulders,
As those slanted bayonets, whole forests of them appearing in the dis-
    tance, approach and pass on, returning homeward,
Moving with steady motion, swaying to and fro to the right and left,
Evenly lightly rising and falling while the steps keep time;
Spirit of hours I knew, all hectic red one day, but pale as death next day,
Touch my mouth ere you depart, press my lips close,
Leave me your pulses of rage—bequeath them to me—fill me with
    currents convulsive,
Let them scorch and blister out of my chants when you are gone,
Let them identify you to the future in these songs.

First O Songs for a Prelude

First O songs for a prelude,
Lightly strike on the stretch'd tympanum pride and joy in my city,
How she led the rest to arms, how she gave the cue,
How at once with lithe limbs unwaiting a moment she sprang,
(O superb! O Manhattan, my own, my peerless!
O strongest you in the hour of danger, in crisis! O truer than steel!)
How you sprang; how you threw off the costumes of peace with
    indifferent hand,
How your soft opera-music changed, and the drum and fife were heard
    in their stead,

How you led to the war. (that shall serve for our prelude, songs of
    soldiers)
How Manhattan drum-taps led.

Forty years had I in my city seen soldiers parading,
Forty years as a pageant, till unawares the lady of this teeming and
    turbulent city, Sleepless amid her ships, her houses, her incalcuable
    wealth,
With her million children around her, suddenly,
At dead of night, at news from the south,
Incens'd struck with chinch'd hand the pavement.

A shock electric, the night sustain'd it,
Till with ominous hum our hive at daybreak pour'd out its myriads.
From the houses then and the workshops, and through all the
    doorways,
Leapt they tumultuous, and lo! Manhattan arming.

Cavalry Crossing a Ford

A line in long array where they wind betwixt green islands,
They take a serpentine course, their arms flash in the sun—hark to the
    musical clank,
Behold the silvery river, in it the splashing horses loitering stop to drink,
Behold the brown-faced men, each group, each person, a picture, the
    negligent rest on the saddles,
Some emerge on the opposite bank, others are just entering the ford-while,
Scarlet and blue and snowy white,
The guidon flags flutter gayly in the wind.

By the Bivouac's Fitful Flame

By the bivouac's fitful flame,
A procession winding around me, solemn and sweet and slow—
    but first I note,
The tents of the sleeping army, the fields' and woods' dim outline,
The darkness lit by spots of kindled fire, the silence,
Like a phantom far or near an occasional figure moving,
The shrubs and trees, (as I lift my eyes they seem to be stealthily
    watching me)
While wind in procession thoughts, O tender and wondrous thoughts,
Of life and death, of home and the past and loved, and of those that are
    far away;
A solemn and slow procession there as I sit on the ground,
By the bivouac's fitful flame.

Come Up From the Fields Father

Come up from the fields father, here's a letter from our Pete,
And come to the front door mother, here's a letter from
    thy dear son.

Lo, 'tis autumn,
Lo, where the trees, deeper green, yellower and redder,
Cool and sweeten Ohio's villages with leaves fluttering in the moderate
    wind,
Where apples ripe in the orchards hang and grapes on the trellis'd vines,
(Smell you the smell of the grapes on the vines?
Smell you the buckweat where the bees were lately buzzing?)

Above all, lo, the sky so calm, so transparent after the rain, and with
    wondrous clouds,
Below too, all calm, all vital and beautiful, and the farm prospers well.

Down in the fields all prospers well,
But now from the fields come father, come at the daughter's call,
And come to the entry mother, to the front door come right away.

Fast as she can she hurries, something ominous, her steps trembling,
She does not tarry to smooth her hair nor adjust her cap.

Open the envelope quickly,
O this is not our son's writing, yet his name is sign'd,
O a strange hand writes for our dear son, O stricken mother's soul!
All swims before her eyes, flashes with black, she catches the main
    words only,
Sentences broken, gunshot wound in the breast, cavalry skirmish, taken
    to hospital,
At present low, but will soon be better.

Ah now the single figure to me,
Amid all teeming and wealthy Ohio with all its cities and farms,
Sickly white in the face and dull in the head, very faint,
By the jamb of a door leans.

Grieve not so, dear mother, (the just-grown daughter speaks through her
    sobs,
The little sisters huddle around speechless and dismay'd)
See, dearest mother, the letter says Pete will soon be better.

Alas poor boy, he will never be better, (nor may-be needs to be better,
    that brave and simple soul)
While they stand at home at the door he is dead already,
The only son is dead.

But the mother needs to be better,
She with thin form presently drest in black,
By day her meals untouch'd, then at night fitfully sleeping, often wak-
    ing,
In the midnight waking, weeping, longing with one deep longIng,
O that she might withdraw unnoticed, silent from life escape and with-
    draw,
To follow, to seek, to be with her dear dead son.

The Wound-Dresser

An old man bending I come among new faces,
Years looking backward resuming in answer to children,
Come tell us old man, as from young men and maidens that love me,
(Arous'd and angry, I'd thought to beat the alarum, and urge relentless war,
But soon my fingers fail'd me, my face droop'd and I resign'd myself,
To sit by the wounded and soothe them, or silently watch the dead)
Years hence of these scenes, of these furious passions, these chances,
Of unsurpass'd heroes (was one side so brave? the other was equally brave)
Now be witness again, paint the mightiest armies of earth,
Of those armies so rapid so wondrous what saw you to tell us?
What stays with you latest and deepest? of curious panics,
Of hard-fought engagements or sieges tremendous what deepest remains?

2

O maidens and young men I love and that love me,
What you ask of my days those the strangest and sudden your talking
    recalls,

Soldier alert I arrive after a long march cover'd with sweat and dust,
In the nick of time I come, plunge in the fight, loudly shout in the rush
    of successful charge,
Enter the captur'd works—yet lo, like a swift-running river they fade,
Pass and are gone they fade—I dwell not on soldiers' perils or
    soldiers' joys,
(Both I remember well, many the hardships, few the joys, yet I was
    content.)

But in silence, in dreams' projections,
While the world of gain and appearance and mirth goes on,
So soon what is over forgotten, and waves wash the imprints off the sand,
With hinged knees returning I enter the doors, (while for you up there,
Whoever you are, follow without noise and be of strong heart.)

Bearing the bandages, Water and sponge,
Straight and swift to my wounded I go,

Where they lie on the ground after the battle brought in,
Where their priceless blood reddens the grass the ground,
Or to the rows of the hospital tent, or under the roof'd hospital,
To the long rows of cots up and down each side I return,
To each and all one after another I draw near, not one do I miss,
An attendant follows holding a tray, he carries a refuse pail,
Soon to be fill'd with clotted rags and blood, emptied, and fill'd again.

I onward go, I stop,
With hinged knees and steady hand to dress wounds,
I am firm with each, the pangs are sharp yet unavoidable,
One turns to me his appealing eyes—poor boy! I never knew you,
Yet I think I could not refuse this moment to die for you, if that would
    save you.

3

On, on I go (open doors of time, open hospital doors!),
The crush'd head I dress (poor crazed hand tear not the bandage away),
The neck of the cavalry-man with the bullet through and through I
    examine,
Hard the breathing rattles, quite glazed already .the eye, yet life
    struggles hard.
(Come sweet death! be persuaded O beautiful death! In mercy come
    quickly.)

From the stump of the arm, the amputated hand,
I undo the clotted lint, remove the slough, wash off the matter and
    blood,
Back on his pillow the soldier bends with curv'd neck and side-falling
    head,
His eyes are closed, his face is pale, he dares not look on the bloody
    stump,
And has not yet look'd on it.

I dress a wound in the side, deep, deep,
But a day or two more, for see the frame all wasted and sinking,
And the yellow-blue countenance see.
I dress the perforated shoulder, the foot with the bullet-wound,

Cleanse the one with a gnawing and putrid gangrene, so sickening, so
    offensive,
While the attendant stands behind aside me holding the tray and pail.

I am faithful, I do not give out,
The fractur'd thigh, the knee, the wound in the abdomen,
These and more I dress with impassive hand, (yet deep in my breast a
    fire, a burning flame.)

4

Thus in silence in dreams' projections,
Returning, resuming, I tread my way through the hospitals,
The hurt and wounded I pacify with soothing hand,
I sit by the restless all the dark night, some are so young,
Some suffer so much, I recall the experience sweet and sad,
(Many a soldier's loving arms about this neck have cross'd and rested,
Many a soldier's kiss dwells on these bearded lips.)

Lo! Victress on the Peaks!

Lo! Victress on the peaks!
Where thou, with mighty brow, regarding the world,
(The world, O Libertad, that vainly conspired against thee;)
Out of its countless beleaguering toils, after thwarting them all;
Dominant, with the dazzling sun around thee,
Flauntest now unharm'd, in immortal soundness and bloom—lo! in
    these hours supreme,
No poem proud,
I, chanting, bring to thee—nor mastery's rapturous verse;
But a book, containing night's darkness, and blood-dripping wounds,
And psalms of the dead

World, Take Good Notice
World, take good notice, silver stars fading,
Milky hue ript, weft of white detaching,
Coals thirty-eight, baleful and burning,
Scarlet, significant, hands off warning,
Now and hencefosth flaunt from these shores.

Thick-Sprinkled Bunting

Thick-Sprinkled bunting! Flag of stars!'
Long yet your road, fateful flag!—long yet your road, and lined with
    bloody death!
For the prize I see at issue, at last is the world
All its ships dnd shores I see, interwoven with your threads, greedy ban-
    ner!
—Dream'd again the flags of kings, highest horn, to flaunt unrival'd?
O hasten, flag of man! O with sure and steady step, passing highest flags
    of kings,
Walk supreme to the heavens, mighty symbol—run up above them all,
Flag of stars! thick-sprinkled bunting!

Song of the Universal
(Commencement Poem, Tuft's College, Mass., June 17,1874)

I

Come, said the Muse,
Sing me a song no poet yet has chanted,
Sing me the Universal.

In this broad Earth of ours,
Amid the measureless grossness and the slag,
Enclosed and safe within its central heart,
Nestles the seed Perfection.

By every life a share, or more or less,
None born but it is born—conceal'd or unconceal'd, the seed is waiting.

2

Lo! keen-eyed, towering Science
As from tall peaks the Modern overlooking,
Successive, absolute fiats issuing.

Forth from their masks, no matter what,
From the huge, festering trunk—from craft and guile and tears,
Health to emerge, and joy—joy universal.

Out of the bulk, the morbid and the shallow
Out of the bad majority—the varied, countless frauds of men and States
Electric, antiseptic yet—cleaving, suffusing all, Only the good is
    universal.

3

Over the mountain growths, disease and sorrow,
An uncaught bird is ever hovering, hovering,
High in the purer; happier air.

From imperfection's murkiest cloud,
Darts always forth one ray of perfect light,
One flash of Heaven's glory.

To fashion's, custom's discord,
To the mad Babel-din, the deafening orgies,
Soothing each lull, a strain is heard, just heard,
From some far shore, the final chorus sounding.

4

O the blest eyes! the happy hearts!
That see—that know the guiding thread so fine,
Along the mighty labyrinth!

5

And thou, America!
For the Scheme's culmination—its Thought, and its Reality,
For these, (not for thyself,)
Thou hast arrived.

Thou too surroundest all;
Embracing, carrying, welcoming all,
Thou too, by pathways broad and new,
To the Ideal tendest.

The measur'd faiths of other lands—the grandeurs of the past,
Are not for Thee—but grandeurs of Thine own;
Deific faiths and amplitudes, absorbing, comprehending all,
All eligible to all.

All, all for Immortality!
Love, like the light, silently wrapping all!
Nature's amelioration blessing all!
The blossoms, fruits of ages—orchards divine and certain;
Forms, objects, growths, humanities, to spiritual Images ripening.

Give me, O God, to sing that thought!
Give me-give him or her I love, this quenchless faith
In thy ensemble. Whatever else withheld, withhold not from us,
Belief in plan of Thee enclosed in Time and Space;
Health, peace, salvation universal.

Is it a dream?
Nay, but the lack of it a dream,
And, failing it, life's lore and wealh a dream,
And all the world a dream.

Long, Too Long, O Land

Long, too long, O land,
Traveling roads all even and peaceful, you learn'd from joys and
    prosperity only;
But now, ah now, to learn from crises of anguish—advancing, grappling
    with direst fate, and recoiling not;.
And now to conceive, and show to the world, what your children
    en-masse really are;
(For who except myself has yet conceiv' d what your children en-masse
    really are?)

Look Down Fair Moon

Look down fair moon, and bathe this scene;
Pour softly down night's nimbus floods, on faces ghastly, swollen, purple;
On the dead, on their backs, with their arms toss'd wide,
Pour down your unstinted nimbus, sacred moon.

Beat! Beat! Drums!

1

Beat! beat! drums!—Blow! bugles! blow!
Through the windows—through doors—burst like a ruthless force,
Into the solemn church, and scatter the congregation;
Into the school where the scholar is studying;
Leave not the bridegroom quiet—no happiness must he have now with
    his bride;
Nor the peaceful farmer any peace, plowing his field or gathering his
    grain;
So fierce you whirr and pound, you drums—so shrill you bugles blow.

2

Beat! beat! drums! Blow! bugles! blow!
Over the traffic of cities—over the rumble of wheels in the streets
Are beds prepared for sleepers at night in the houses?
No sleepers must sleep in those beds;
No bargainers' bargains by day—no brokers or speculators—Would they
    continue?
Would the talkers be talking? Would the singer attempt to sing?
Would the lawyer rise in the court to state his case before the judge?
Then rattle quicker, heavier drums—you bugles wilder blow.

3

Beat! beat! drums!—Blow! bugles! blow!
Make no parley—stop for no expostulation;
Mind not the timid—mind not the weeper or prayer;
Mind not the old man beseeching the young man;
Let not the child's voice be heard, nor the mother's entreaties;
Make even the trestles to shake the dead, where they lie awaiting the
    hearses,
So strong you thump, O terrible drums—so loud you bugles blow.

From Paumanok Starting I Fly Like a Bird

From Paumanock starting, I fly like a bird,
Around and around to soar, to sing the idea of all;
To the north betaking myself, to sing there arctic songs,
To Kanada, till I absorb Kanada in myself—to Michigan then,
To Wisconsin, Iowa, Minnesota, to sing their songs, (they are
    inimitable;)
Then to Ohio and Indiana to sing theirs—to Missouri and Kansas and
    Arkansas, to sing theirs,
To Tennessee and Kentucky-to the Carolinas and Georgia, to sing theirs,
To Texas, and so along up toward California, to roam accepted
    everywhere;
To sing first, (to the tap of the war-drum, if need be)
The idea of all—of the western world, one and inseparable.
And then the song of each member of These States.

Rise O Days, From Your Fathomless Deeps

Rise, O days, from your fathomless deeps, till you loftier, fiercer sweep
Long for my soul, hungering gymnastic, I devour' d what the earth
     gave me;
Long I roam'd the woods of the north—long I watch'd Niagara pouring;
I travel'd the prairies over, and slept on their breast—I cross'd the
     Nevadas, I cross'd the plateaus;
I ascended the towering rocks along the Pacific, I sail'd out to sea;
I sail'd through the storm, I was refresh'd by the storm;
I watch'd with joy the threatening maws of the waves;
I mark'd the white combs where they career'd so high, curling

Memories of President Lincoln

꧁꧂

When Lilacs Last in the Dooryard Bloom'd

1

When lilacs last in the dooryard bloom'd,
And the great star early droop'd in the western sky in the night,
I mourn'd, and yet shall mourn with ever-returning spring.

Ever-returning spring trinity sure to me you bring,
Lilac blooming perennial and drooping star in the west,
And thought of him I love.

2

O powerful western fallen star!
O shades of night—O moody, tearful night!
O great star disappear'd—O the black murk that hides the star!
O cruel hands that hold me powerless—O helpless soul of me!
O harsh surrounding cloud that will not free my soul.

3
In the dooryard fronting an old farm-house near the white-wash'd palings,
Stands the lilac-bush tall-growing with heart-shaped leaves of rich green,
With many a pointed blossom rising delicate, with the perfume strong
    I love,
With every leaf a miracle—and from this bush in the dooryard,
With delicate-color'd blossom and heart-shaped leaves of rich green,
A spring with its flower I break.

4

In the swamp in secluded recesses,
A shy and hidden bird is warbling a song.

Solitary the thrush,
The hermit withdrawn to himself, avoiding the settlements,
Sings by himself a song.

Song of the bleeding throat,
Death's outlet song of life, (for well dear brother I know,
If thou wast not granted to sing thou would'st surely die.)

5

Over the breast of the spring, the land, amid cities,
Amid lanes and through old woods, where lately the violets peep'd
    from the ground, spotting the gray debris,
Amid the grass in the fields each side of the lanes, passing the
    endless grass,
Passing the yellow-spear'd wheat, every grain from its shroud in the
    dark-brown fields uprisen,
Passing the apple-tree blows of white and pink in the orchards,
Carrying a corpse to where it shall rest in the grave,
Night and day journeys a coffin.

6

Coffin that passes through lanes and streets,
Through day and night with the great cloud darkening the land,
With the pomp of the inloop'd flags with the cities draped in black,
With the show of the States themselves as of crape-veil'd women standing,
With processions long and winding and the flambeaus of the night,
With the countless torches lit, with the silent sea of faces and the
    unbared heads,
With the waiting depot, the arriving coffin, and the sombre faces,
With dirges through the night, with the thousand voices rising strong
    and solemn,
With all the mournful voices of the dirges pour'd around the coffin,

The dim-lit churches and the shuddering organs—where amid these
    you journey,
With the tolling tolling bells' perpetual clang,
Here, coffin that slowly passes,
I give you my sprig of lilac.

7

(Nor for you, for one alone,
Blossoms and branches green to coffins all I bring,
For fresh as the morning, thus would I chant a song for you O sane and
    sacred death.
All over bouquets of roses,
O death, I cover you over with roses and early lilies,
But mostly and now the lilac that blooms the first,
Copious I break, I break the sprigs from the bushes,
With loaded arms I come, pouring for you,
For you and the coffins all of you O death.)

8

O western orb sailing the heaven,
Now I know what you must have meant as a month since I walk'd,
As I walk'd in silence the transparent shadowy night,
As I saw you had something to tell as you bent to me night after night,
As you droop'd from the sky low down as if to my side, (while the other
    stars all look'd on)
As we wander'd together the solemn night, (for something I know not
    what kept me from sleep)
As the night advanced, and I saw on the rim of the west how full you
    were of woe,
As I stood on the rising ground in the breeze in the cool transparent night,
As I watch'd where you pass'd and was lost in the netherward black of
    the night,
As my soul in its trouble dissatisfied sank, as where you sad orb,
Concluded, dropt in the night, and was gone.

9

Sing on there in the swamp,
O singer bashful and tender, I hear your notes, I hear your call,
I hear, I come presently, I understand you,
But a moment I linger, for the lustrous star has detain'd me,
The star my departing comrade holds and detains me.

10

O how shall I warble myself for the dead one there I loved?
And how shall I deck my song for the large sweet soul that has gone?
And what shall my perfume be for the grave of him I love?
Sea-winds blown from east and west,
Blown from the Eastern sea and blown from the Western sea, till there
    on the prairies meeting,
These and with these and the breath of my chant,
I'll perfume the grave of him I love.

11

O what shall I hang on the chamber walls?
And what shall the pictures be that I hang on the walls,
To adorn the burial-house of him I love?

Pictures of growing spring and farms and homes,
With the Fourth-month eve at sundown, and the gray smoke lucid
    and bright,
With floods of the yellow gold of the gorgeous, indolent, sinking sun,
    burning, expanding the air,
With the fresh sweet herbage under foot, and the pale green leaves of
    the trees prolific,
In the distance the flowing glaze, the breast of the river, with a wind-
    dapple here and there,
With ranging hills on the banks, with many a line against the sky, and
    shadows,
And the city at hand with dwellings so dense, and stacks of chimneys,
And all the scenes of life and the workshops, and the workmen
    homeward returning.

12

Lo, body and soul—this land,
My own Manhattan with spires, and the sparkling and hurrying tides,
    and the ships,
The varied and ample land, the South and the North in the light, Ohio's
    shores and flashing Missouri,
And ever the far-spreading prairies cover'd with grass and corn.

Lo, the most excellent sun so calm and haughty,
The violet and purple mom with just-felt breezes,
The gentle soft-born measureless light,
The miracle spreading bathing all, the fulfill'd noon,
The coming eve delicious, the welcome night and the stars,
Over my cities shining all, enveloping man and land.

13

Sing on, sing on you gray-brown bird,
Sing from the swamps, the recesses, pour your chant from the bushes,
Limitless out of the dusk, out of the cedars and pines.

Sing on dearest brother, warble your reedy song,
Loud human song, with voice of uttermost woe.

O liquid and free and tender!
O wild and loose to my soul—O wondrous singer!

You only I hear—yet the star holds me (but will soon depart),
Yet the lilac with mastering odor holds me.

14

Now while I sat in the day and look'd forth,
In the close of the day with its light and the fields of spring, and the
    farmers preparing their crops,
In the large unconscious scenery of my land with its lakes and forests,
In the heavenly aerial beauty, (after the perturb'd winds and the storms)

Under the arching heavens of the afternoon swift passing, and the voices
    of children and women,
The many-moving sea-tides, and I saw the ships how they sail'd,
And the summer approaching with richness, and the fields all busy with
    labor,
And the infinite separate houses, how they all went on, each with its
    meals and minutia of daily usages,
And the streets how their throbbings throbb'd, and the cities pent—
    lo, then and there,
Falling upon them all and among them all, enveloping me with the rest,
Appear'd the cloud, appear'd the long black trail,
And I knew death, its thought, and the sacred knowledge of death.

Then with the knowledge of death as walking one side of me,
And the thought of death close-walking the other side of me,
And I in the middle as with companions, and as holding the hands of
    companions,
I fled forth to the hiding receiving night that talks not,
Down to the shores of the water, the path by the swamp in the dimness,
To the solemn shadowy cedars and ghostly pines so still.

And the singer so shy to the rest receiv'd me,
The gray-brown bird I know receiv'd us comrades three,
And he sang the carol of death, and a verse for him I love.

From deep secluded recesses,
From the fragrant cedars and the ghostly pines so still,
Came the carol of the bird.

And the charm of the carol rapt me,
As I held as if by their hands my comrades in the night,
And the voice of my spirit tallied the song of the bird.

Come lovely and soothing death,
Undulate round the world, serenely arriving, arriving,
In the day, in the night, to all, to each,
Sooner or later delicate death.

Prais'd be the fathomless universe,

For life and joy, and for objects and knowledge curious,
And for love, sweet love—but praise! praise! praise!
For the sure-enwinding arms of cool-enfolding death.
Dark mother always gliding near with soft feet,
Have none chanted for thee a chant of fullest welcome?
Then I chant it for thee, I glorify thee above all,
I bring thee a song that when thou must indeed come, come unfalteringly.

Approach strong deliveress,
When it is so, when thou hast taken them I joyously sing the dead,
Lost in the loving floating ocean of thee,
Laved in the flood of thy bliss O death.

From me to thee glad serenades,
Dances for thee I propose saluting thee, adornments and feastings for thee,
And the sights of the open landscape and the high-spread sky are fitting,
And life and the fields, and the huge and thoughtful night.

The night in silence under many a star,
The ocean shore and the husky whispering wave whose voice I know,
And the soul turning to thee O vast and well-veil'd death,
And the body gratefully nestling close to thee.

Over the tree-tops I float thee a song,
Over the rising and sinking waves, over the myriad fields and the prairies wide,
Over the dense-pack'd cities all and the teeming wharves and ways,
I float this carol with joy, with joy to thee O death.

15

To the tally of my soul,
Loud and strong kept up the gray-brown bird,
With pure deliberate notes spreading filling the night.

Loud in the pines and cedars dim,
Clear in the freshness moist and the swamp-perfume,
And I with my comrades there in the night.

While my sight that was bound in my eyes unclosed,

As to long panoramas of visions.

And I saw askant the armies,
I saw as in noiseless dreams hundreds of battle-flags,
Bome through the smoke of the battles and pierc'd with missiles I saw
    them,
And carried hither and yon through the smoke, and torn and bloody,
And at last but a few shreds left on the staffs (and all in silence),
And the staffs all splinter'd and broken.

I saw battle-corpses, myriads of them,
And the white skeletons of young men, I saw them,
I saw the debris and debris of all the slain soldiers of the war,
But I saw they were not as was thought,
They themselves were fully at rest, they suffered not,
The living remain'd and suffered, the mother suffered,
And the wife and the child and the musing comrade suffered,
And the armies that remain'd suffer'd.

16

Passing the visions, passing the night,
Passing, unloosing the hold of my comrades' hands,

Passing the song of the hermit bird and the tallying song of my soul,
Victorious song, death's outlet song, yet varying ever-altering song,
As low and wailing, yet clear the notes, rising and falling, flooding the
    night,
Sadly sinking and fainting, as warning and warning, and yet again burst-
    ing with joy,
Covering the earth and filling the spread of the heaven,
As that powerful psalm in the night I heard from recesses,
Passing, I leave thee lilac with heart-shaped leaves,
I leave thee there in the door-yard, blooming, returning with spring.

I cease from my song for thee,
From my gaze on thee in the west, fronting the west, communing with
    thee,
O comrade lustrous with silver face in the night.

Yet each to keep and all, retrievements out of the night,
The song, the wondrous chant of the gray-brown bird,
And the tallying chant, the echo arous'd in my soul,
With the lustrous and drooping star with the countenance full of woe,
With the holders holding my hand nearing the call of the bird,
Comrades mine and I in the midst, and their memory ever to keep, for
    the dead I loved so well,
For the sweetest, wisest soul of all my days and lands—and this for his
    dear sake, Lilac and star and bird twined with the chant of my soul,
There in the fragrant pines and the cedars dusk and dim.

O Captain! My Captain!
(Abraham Lincoln, 1809–1865)

O Captain! my Captain! our fearful trip is done,
The ship has weather'd every rack, the prize we sought is won,
The port is near, the bells I hear, the people all exulting,
While follow eyes the steady keel, the vessel grim and daring;
    But O heart! heart! heart!
     O the bleeding drops of red,
       Where on the deck my Captain lies,
       Fallen cold and dead.

O Captain! my Captain! rise up and hear the bells;
Rise up—for you the flag is flung—for you the bugle trills,
For you bouquets and ribbon'd wreaths—for you the shores a-crowding,
For you they call, the swaying mass, their eager faces turning;
    Here Captain! dear father!
     This arm beneath your head!
      It is some dream that on the deck,
       You've fallen cold and dead.

My Captain does not answer, his lips are pale and still,
My father does not feel my arm, he has no pulse nor will,
The ship is anchor'd safe and sound, its voyage closed and done,
From fearful trip the victor ship comes in with object won;
    Exult O shores, and ring O bells!
     But I with mournful tread,
      Walk the deck my Captain lies
       Fallen cold and dead.

Hush'd Be The Camps Today
(May 4, 1865)

Hush'd be the camps to-day,
And soldiers let us drape our war-worn weapons,
And each with musing soul retire to celebrate,
Our dear commander's death.

No more for him life's stormy conflicts,
Nor victory, nor defeat—no more time's dark events,
Charging like ceaseless clouds across the sky.

But sing poet in our name,
Sing of the love we bore him—because you, dweller in camps, know
    it truly.

As they invault the coffin there,
Sing—as they close the doors of the earth upon him—one verse,
For the heavy hearts of soldiers.

Nature, Man and Self

❦

To the Man-of War Bird

Thou who hast slept all night upon the storm,
Waking renew'd on thy prodigious pinions,
(Burst the wild storm? above it thou ascended'st
And rested on the sky, thy slave that cradled thee),
Now a blue point, far, far in heaven floating,
As to the light emerging here on deck I watch thee.
(Myself a speck, a point on the world's floating vast.)

Far, far at sea,
After the night's fierce drifts have strewn the shore with wrecks,
With re-appearing day as now so happy and serene,
The rosy and elastic dawn, the flashing sun,
The limpid spread of air cerulean,
Thou also re-appearest.

Thou born to match the gale, (thou art all wings)
To cope with heaven and earth and sea and hurricane,
Thou ship of air that never furl'st thy sails,
Days, even weeks untired and onward, through spaces, realms gyrating,
At dusk that look'st on Senegal, at morn America,
That sport'st amid the lightningflash and thunder-cloud,
In them, in thy experiences, had'st thou my soul,
What joys! what joys were thine!

A Paumanok Picture

Two boats with nets lying off the sea-beach, quite still,
Ten fishermen waiting—they discover a thick school of mossbonkers—
    they drop the join'd seine-ends in the water,
The boats separate and row off, each on its rounding course to the
    beach, enclosing the mossbonkers,
The net is drawn in by a windlass by those who stop ashore,
Some of the fishermen lounge in their boats, others stand ankle-deep in
    the water, pois'd on strong legs,
The boats partly drawn up, the water slapping against them,
Strew'd on the sand in heaps and windrows,
well out from the water, the green-back'd spotted mossbonkers.

Patroling Barnegat

Wild, wild the storm, and the sea high running,
Steady the roar of the gale, with incessant undertone muttering,
Shouts of demoniac laughter fitfully piercing and pealing,
Waves, air, midnight, their savagest trinity lashing,
Out in the shadows there milk-white combs careering,
On beachy slush and sand spirts of snow fierce slanting,
Where through the murk the easterly death-wind breasting,
Through cutting swirl and spray watchful and firm advancing,
(That in the distance! is that a wreck? is the red signal flaring?)

Slush and sand of the beach tireless till daylight wending,
Steadily, slowly, through hoarse roar never remitting,
Along the midnight edge by those milk-white combs careering,
A group of dim, weird forms, struggling, the night confronting,
That savage trinity warily watching.

Old Salt Kossabone

Far back, related on my mother's side,
Old Salt Kossabone, I'll tell you how he died:
(Had been a sailor all his life—was nearly 90—lived with his
    married grandchild, Jenny;
House on a hill, with view of bay at hand, and distant cape, and
    stretch to open sea;)
The last of afternoons, the evening hours, for many a year his
    regular custom,
In his great arm chair by the window seated,
(Sometimes, indeed, through half the day)
Watching the coming, going of the vessels, he mutters to
    himself—And now the close of all:
One struggling outbound brig, one day, baffled for long—
    cross-tides and much wrong going,
At last at nightfall strikes the breeze aright, her whole luck veering,
And swiftly bending round the cape, the darkness proudly entering,
    cleaving, as be watches,
"She's free—she's on her destination"—these the last words—
    when Jenny came, he sat there dead,
Dutch Kossabone, Old Salt, related on my mother's side, far back.

With Husky Haughty Lips, O Sea!

With husky-haughty lips, O sea!
Where day and night I wend thy surf-beat shore,
Imaging to my sense thy varied strange suggestions
(I see and plainly list thy talk and conference here),
Thy troops of white-maned racers racing to the goal,
Thy ample, smiling face, dash'd with the sparkling dimples of the sun,
Thy brooding scowl and murk—thy unloos'd hurricanes,
Thy unsubduedness caprices, wilfulness;
Great as thou art above the rest, thy many tears—a lack from all eternity
    in thy content,
(Naught but the greatest struggles, wrongs, defeats, could make thee
    greatest—no less could make thee)
Thy lonely state—something thou ever seek'st and seek'st, yet never
    gain'st,
Surely some right withheld—some voice, in huge monotonous rage, of
    freedom lover pent,
Some vast heart, like a planet's, chain'd and chafing in those breakers,

By lengthen'd swell, and spasm, and panting breath,
And rhythmic rasping of thy sands and waves,
And serpent hiss, and savage peals of laughter
And undertones of distant lion roar,
(Sounding, appealing to the sky's deaf ear—but now rapport for once,
A phantom in the night thy confidant for once)
The first and last confession of the globe,
Outsurging, muttering from thy soul's abysms,
The tale of cosmic elemental passion,
Thou tellest to a kindred soul.

To The Sun-Set Breeze

Ah, whispering, something again, unseen,
Where late this heated day thou enterest at my window, door,
Thou, laying, tempering all, cool-freshing, gently vitalizing
Me, old, alone, sick, weak-down, melted-worn with sweat;
Thou, nestling, folding close and firm yet soft, companion better than
    talk, book, art,
(Thou hast, O Nature! elements! utterance to my heart beyond the
    rest—and this is of them)
So sweet thy primitive taste to breathe within—thy soothing fingers on
    my face and hands,
Thou, messenger-magical strange bringer to body and spirit of me,
(Distances balk'd—occult medicines penetrating me from head to foot)
I feel the sky, the prairies vast—I feel the mighty northern lakes,
I feel the ocean and the forest—somehow I feel the globe itself
    swift-swimming in space;
Thou blown from lips so loved, now gone—haply from endless store,
    God-sent,
(For thou art spiritual, Godly, most of all known to my sense)
Minister to speak to me, here and now, what word has never told, and
    cannot tell,
Art thou not universal concrete's distillation? Law's all Astronomy's last
    refinement?
Hast thou no soul? Can I not know, identity thee?

From Far Dakota's Canons
(June 25, 1876)

From far Dakota's canons,
Lands of the wild ravine, the dusky Sioux, the lonesome stretch,
    the silence,
Haply to-day a mournful wail, haply a trumpet-note for heroes.

The battle-bulletin,
The Indian ambuscade, the craft, the fatal environment,
The cavalry companies fighting to the last in sternest heroism,
In the midst of their little circle, with their slaughter'd horses for
    breastworks,
The fall of Custer and all his officers and men.

Continues yet the old, old legend of our race,
The loftiest of life upheld by death,
The ancient banner perfectly maintain'd,
O lesson opportune, O how I welcome thee!

As sitting in dark days,
Lone, sulky, through the time's thick murk looking in vain for light,
    for hope,
From unsuspected parts a fierce and momentary proof,
(The sun there at the centre though conceal'd
Electric life forever at the centre),
Breaks forth a lightning flash.

Thou of the tawny flowing hair in battle,
I erewhile saw, with erect head, pressing ever in front, bearing a
    bright sword in thy hand,
Now ending well in death the splendid fever of thy deeds
(I bring no dirge for it or thee, I bring a glad triumphal sonnet),
Desperate and glorious, aye in defeat most desperate, most glorious,
After thy many battles in which never yielding up a gun or a color,
Leaving behind thee a memory sweet to soldiers,
Thou yieldest up thyself.

The Dead Tenor

As down the stage again,
With Spanish hat and plumes, and gait inimitable,
Back from the fading lessons of the past. I'd call, I'd tell and own,
How much from thee! the revelation of the singing voice from thee!
(So firm—so liquid-soft—again that tremulous, manly timbre!
The perfect singing voice—deepest of all to me the lesson—trial and
    test of all:)
How through those strains distill'd—how the rapt ears, the soul of me,
    absorbing
Fernando's heart, *Manrico's* passionate call, *Ernani's,* sweet *Gennaro's,*
I fold thenceforth, or seek to fold, within my chants transmuting,
Freedom's and Love's and Faith's unloos'd cantabile,
(As perfume's color's, sunlight's correlation:)
From these, for these, with these, a hurried line, dead tenor,
A wafted autumn leaf, dropt in the closing grave, the shovel'd earth,
To memory of thee.

Prayer of Columbus

A batter'd, wreck'd old man,
Thrown on this savage shore, far, far from home,
Pent by the sea and dark rebellious brows, twelve dreary months,
Sore, stiff with many toils, sicken'd and nigh to death,
I take my way along the island's edge,
Venting a heavy heart.

I am too full of woe!
Haply I may not live another day;
I cannot rest O God, I cannot eat or drink or sleep,
Till I put forth myself, my prayer, once more to Thee,
Breathe, bathe myself once more in Thee, commune with Thee,
Report myself once more to Thee.

Thou knowest my years entire, my life,
My long and crowded life of active work, not adoration merely;
Thou knowest the prayers and vigils of my youth,
Thou knowest my manhood's solemn and visionary meditations,
Thou knowest how before I commenced I devoted all to come to Thee,
Thou knowest I have in age ratified all those vows and strictly kept them,
Thou knowest I have not once lost nor faith nor ecstasy in Thee,

In shackles, prison'd, in disgrace, repining not,
Accepting all from Thee, as duly come from Thee.

All my emprises have been fill'd with Thee,
My speculations, plans, begun and carried on in thoughts of Thee,
Sailing the deep or journeying the land for Thee;
Intentions, purports, aspirations mine, leaving results to
Thee,

O I am sure they really came from Thee,
The urge, the ardor, the unconquerable will,
The potent, felt, interior command, stronger than words,
A message from the Heavens whispering to me even in sleep,
These sped me on.

By me and these the work so far accomplish'd,
By me earth's elder cloy'd and stifled lands uncloy'd, unloos'd,
By me the hemispheres rounded and tied, the unknown to the known.

The end I know not, it is all in Thee,
Or small or great I know not—haply what broad fields, what lands,
Haply the brutish measureless human undergrowth I know,
Transplanted there may rise to stature, knowledge worthy Thee,
Haply the swords I know may there be turn'd to reaping tools,
Haply the lifeless cross I know, Europe's dead cross, may bud and
    blossom there.

One effort more, my altar this bleak sand;
That Thou O God my life hast lighted,
With ray of light, steady, ineffable, vouchsafed of Thee,
Light rare untellable, lighting the very light,
Beyond all signs, descriptions, languages;
For that O God, be it my latest word, here on my knees,
Old, poor, and paralyzed, I thank Thee.

My terminus near,
The clouds already closing in upon me,
The voyage balk'd, the course disputed, lost,
I yield my ships to Thee.

My hands, my limbs grow nerveless.
My brain feels rack'd, bewilder'd,
Let the old timbers part, I will not part,
I will cling fast to Thee, O God, though the waves buffet me,
Thee, Thee at least I know.

Is it the prophet's thought I speak, or am I raving?
What do I know of life? what of myself?
I know not even my own work past or present,
Dim ever-shifting guesses of it spread before me,
Of newer better worlds, their mighty parturition,
Mocking, perplexing me.

And these things I see suddenly, what mean they?
As if some miracle, some hand divine unseal'd my eyes,
Shadowy vast shapes smile through the air and sky,
And on the distant waves sail countless ships,
And anthems in new tongues I hear saluting me.

Old Ireland

Far hence amid an isle of wondrous beauty,
Crouching over a grave an ancient sorrowful mother,
Once a queen, now lean and tatter'd seated on the ground,
Her old white hair drooping dishevel'd round her shoulders,
At her feet fallen an unused royal harp,
Long silent, she too long silent, mourning her shrouded hope and heir,
Of all the earth her heart roost full of sorrow because most full of love.

Yet a word ancient mother,
You need crouch there no longer on the cold ground with forehead
    between your knees,
O you need not sit there veil'd in your old white hair so dishevel'd,
For know you the one you mourn is not in that grave,
It was an illusion, the son you love was not really dead,
The Lord is not dead, he is risen again young and strong in another
    country,
Even while you wept there by your fallen harp by the grave,
What you wept for was translated, pass'd from the grave,
The winds favor'd and the sea sail'd it,
And now with rosy and new blood,
Moves to-day in a new country.

O Star of France
(1870–71)

O Star of France,
The brightness of thy hope and strength and fame,
Like some proud ship that led the fleet so long,
Beseems to-day a wreck driven by the gale, a mastless hulk,
And 'mid its teeming madden'd half-drown'd crowds,
Nor helm nor helmsman.

Dim smitten Star,
Orb not of France alone, pale symbol of my soul, its dearest hopes,
The struggle and the daring, rage divine for liberty,
Of aspirations toward the far ideal, enthusiast's dreams of brotherhood.
Of terror to the tyrant and the priest.

Star crucified—by traitors sold,
Star panting o'er a land of death, heroic land,
Strange, passionate, mocking, frivolous land.

Miserable yet for thy errors, vanities, sins, I will not now rebuke thee,
Thy unexampled woes and pangs have quell'd them all,
And left thee sacred.

In that amid thy many faults thou ever aimedst highly,
In that thou wouldst not really sell thyself however great the price,
In that thou surely wakedst weeping from thy drugg'd sleep,
In that alone amongthy sisters thou, giantess, didst rend the ones that
    shamed thee,
In that thou couldst not, wouldst not, wear the usual chains,
This cross, thy livid face,
thy pierced bands and feet,
The spear thrust in thy side.

O star! O ship of France, beat back and baffled long!
Bear up O Smitten orb! O ship continue on!

Sure as the ship of all, the Earth itself,
Product of deathly fire and turbulent chaos,
Forth from its spasms of fury and its poisons,
Issuing at last in perfect power and beauty,
Onward beneath the sun following its course,
So thee O ship of France!

Finish'd the days, the clouds dispel'd,
The travail o'er, the long-sought extrication,
When lo! reborn, high o'er the European world,
(In gladness answering thence, as face afar to face, reflecting ours
    Columbia)
Again thy star O France, fair lustrous star,
In heavenly peace, clearer, more bright than ever.
Shall beam immortal.

The Justified Mother of Men

The old face of the mother of many children,
Whist! I am fully content.

Lull'd and late is the smoke of the First-day morning,
It hangs low over the rows of trees by the fences.
It hangs thin by the sassafras and wild-cherry and cat-brier under them.
I saw the rich ladies in full dress at the soiree,
I heard what the singers were singing so long,
Heard who sprang in crimson youth from the white froth and the
    water-blue.

Behold a woman!
She looks out from her quaker cap, her face is clearer and more
    beautiful than the sky.

She sits in an armchair under the shaded porch of the farmhouse,
The sun just shines on her old white head.

Her ample gown is of cream-hued linen,
Her grandsons raised the flax, and her grand-daughters spun it with the
    distaff and the wheel.

The melodious character of the earth,
The finish beyond which philosophy cannot go and does not wish to go,
The justified mother of men.

Spirit that Form'd this Scene
(Written in Platte Canyon, Colorado)

Spirit that form'd this scene,
These tumbled rock-piles grim and red,
These reckless heaven-ambitious peaks,
These gorges, turbulent-clear streams, this naked freshness,
These formless wild arrays, for reasons of their own,
I know thee, savage spirit—we have communed together,
Mine too such wild arrays, for reasons of their own;
Was't charged against my chants they had forgotten art?
To fuse within themselves its rules precise and delicatesse?
The lyrist's measur'd beat, the wrought-out temple's grace—column and
    polish'd arch forgot?
But thou that revelest here—spirit that form'd this scene.
They have remember'd thee.

When I Heard the Learn'd Astronomer

When I heard the learn'd astronomer,
When the proofs, the figures, were ranged in columns before me,
When I was shown the charts and diagrams, to add, divide,
    and measure them,
When I sitting heard the astronomer where he lectured
    with much applause in the lecture-room,
How soon unaccountable I became tired and sick,
Till rising and gliding out I wander'd off by myself,
In the mystical moist night-air, and from time to time,
Look'd up in perfect silence at the stars.

Out From Behind This Mask
(To Confront a Portrait)

Out from behind this bending rough-cut mask,
These lights and shades, this drama of the whole,
This common curtain of the lace contain'd in me for me, in
    you for you, in each for each,
(Tragedies, sorrows, laughter, tears—O heaven!
The passionate teeming plays this curtain hid!)
This glaze of God's serenest purest sky,
This film of Satan's seething pit,
This heart's geography's map, this limitless small continent, this
    soundless sea;
Out from the convolutions of this globe,
This subtler astronomic orb than sun or moon, than Jupiter, Venus, Mars,
This condensation of the universe, (nay here the only universe,
Here the idea, all in this mystic handful wrapt;)
These burin'd eyes, flashing to you to pass to future time,
To launch and spin through space revolving sideling, from these to
    emanate,
To you whoe'er you are—a look.

2

A traveler of thoughts and years, of peace and war,
Of youth long sped and middle age declining,
(As the first volume of a tale perused and laid away, and this the second,
Songs, ventures, speculations, presently to close)
Lingering a moment here and now, to you I opposite turn,
As on the road or at some crevice door by chance, or open'd window,
Pausing, inclining, baring my head, you specially I greet,
To draw and clinch your soul for once inseparably with mine,
Then travel travel on.

Recorders Ages Hence

Recorders ages hence,
Come, I will take you down underneath this impassive exterior, I will
    tell you what to say of me,
Publish my name and bang up my picture as that of the tenderest lover.
The friend the lover's portrait, of whom his friend his lover was fondest,
Who was not proud of his songs, but of the measureless ocean of love
    within him, and freely pour'd it forth,
Who often walk'd lonesome walks thinking of his dear friends, his lovers,
Who pensive away from one he lov'd often lay sleepless and dissatisfied
    at night,
Who knew too well the sick, sick dread lest the one he lov'd might
    secretly be indifferent to him,
Whose happiest days were far away through fields, in
woods, on hills, he and another wandering hand in hand, they twain
    apart from other men,
Who oft as he saunter'd the streets curv'd with his arm the shoulder of
    his friend, while the arm of his friend rested upon him also.

By Broad Potomac's Shore

By broad Potomac's shore, again old tongue,
(Still uttering, still ejaculating, canst never cease this babble?)
Again old heart so gay, again to you, your sense, the full flush spring
    returning,
Again the freshness and the odors, again Virginia's summer sky, pellucid
    blue and silver,
Again the forenoon purple of the hills,
Again the deathless grass, so noiseless soft and green,
Again the blood-red roses blooming.

Perfume this book of mine O blood-red roses!
Lave subtly with your waters every line Potomac!
Give me of you O spring, before I close, to put between its pages!
O forenoon purple of the hills, before I close, of you!
O deathless grass, of you!

Song for All Seas, All Ships

Today a rude brief recitative,
Of ships sailing the seas, each with its special flag or ship-signal,
Of unnamed heroes in the ships—of waves spreading and spreading far
    as the eye can reach,
Of dashing spray, and the winds piping and blowing,
And out of these a chant for the sailors of all nations,
Fitful, like a surge.

Of sea-captains young or old, and the mates, and of all intrepid sailors,
Of the few, very choice, taciturn, whom fate can never surprise nor
    death dismay,
Picked sparingly without noise by thee, old ocean, chosen by thee,
Thou sea that pickest and cullest the race in time, and unitest nations,
Suckled by thee, old husky nurse, embodying thee, Indomitable,
    untamed as thee.

(Ever the heroes on water or on land, by ones or twos appearing,
Ever the stock preserved and never lost, though rare, enough for seed
    preserved.)

II

Flaunt out, O sea, your separate flags of nations!
Flaunt out visible as ever the various ship-signals!
But do you reserve especially for yourself and for the soul of man one
    flag above all the rest,
A spiritual woven signal for all nations, emblem of man elate above death.

The Last Invocation

At the last, tenderly,
From the walls of the powerful, fortressed house,
From the clasp of the knitted locks, from the keep of the
    well-closed doors,
Let me be wafted.

Let me glide noiselessly forth;
With the key of softness unlock the locks—with a whisper
Set ope the doors, O soul!

Tenderly—be not impatient!
(Strong is your hold, O mortal flesh!
Strong is your hold, O love!)

I Saw in Louisiana a Live-Oak Growing

I saw in Louisiana a live-oak growing,
All alone flood it, and the moss hung down from the branches;
Without any companion it grew there, uttering joyous leaves of
    dark green,
And its look, rude, unbending, lusty, made me think of myself;
But I wonder'd how it could utter joyous leaves, standing alone there,
    without its friend, its lover near—for I knew I could not;
And I broke off a twig with a certain number of leaves upon it, and
    twined around it a little moss,
And brought it away—and I have placed it in sight in my room;
It is not needed to remind me as of my own dear, friends,
(For I believe lately I think of little else than of them:)
Yet it remains to me a curious token—it makes me think of manly love;
For all that, and though the live-oak glistens there in Louisiana, solitary,
    in a wide flat space,
Uttering joyous leaves all its life, without a friend, a lover, near,
I know very well I could not.

Demon or bird (said the boy's soul)
Is it indeed toward your mate you sing? or is it really to me?
For I, that was a child, my tongue's use sleeping, now I have heard you,
Now in a moment I know what I am for, I awake,
And already a thousand singers, a thousand songs, clearer, louder and
    more sorrowful than yours,
A thousand warbling echoes have started to life within me,
    never to die.

O you singer solitary, singing by yourself, projecting me,
O solitary me listening, never more shall I cease perpetuating you,
Never more shall I escape, never more the reverberations,
Never more the cries of unsatisfied love be absent from me,
Never again leave me to be the peaceful child I was before what there in
    the night,
By the sea under the yellow and sagging moon,
The messenger there aroused, the fire, the sweet hell within,
The unknown want, the destiny of me.

O give me the clew! (It lurks in the night here somewhere)
O if I am to have so much, let me have more!

A word then, (for I will conquer it)
The word final, superior to all,
Subtle, sent up—what is it?—I listen;
Are you whispering it, and have been all the time, you sea-waves?
Is that it from your liquid rims and wet sands?

Whereto answering, the sea,
Delaying not, hurrying not,
Whispered me through the night, and very plainly before daybreak,
Lisped to me the low and delicious word death,
And again death, death, death, death,
Hissing melodious, neither like the bird' nor like my aroused child's heart,
But edging near as privately for me, rustling at my feet,
Creeping thence steadily up to my ears and laving me softly all over,
Death, death, death, death, death.

Which I do not forget,
But fuse the song of my dusky demon and brother,
That he sang to me in the moonlight on Paumanok's
    gray beach,

With the thousand responsive songs at random;
My own songs awaked from that hour,
And with them the key, the word up from the waves,
The word of the sweetest song and all song's,
That strong and delicious word which, creeping to my feet,
(Or like some old crone rocking the cradle, swathed in sweet garments,
    bending aside)
The sea whispered me.

Token of all brave captains and all intrepid sailors and mates,
And all that went down doing their duty,
Reminiscent of them, twined from all intrepid captains young or old,
A pennant universal, subtly waving all time, o'er all brave sailors,
All seas, all ships.

As Toilsome I Wandered Virginia's Woods

As toilsome I wandered Virginia's woods,
To the music of rustling leaves kicked by my feet, (for 'twas autumn)
I marked at the foot of a tree the grave of a soldier;
Mortally wounded he and buried on the retreat, (easily all could I
    understand)
The halt of a mid-day hour, when up! no time to lose—yet this sign left,
On a tablet scrawled and nailed on the tree by the grave,
Bold, cautious, true, and my loving comrade.

Long, long I muse, then on my way go wandering,
Many a changeful season to follow, and many a scene of life,
Yet at times through changeful season and scene, abrupt, alone, or in the
    crowded street,
Comes before me the unknown soldier's grave, comes the inscription
    rude in Virginia's woods,
Bold, cautious, true, and my loving comrade.

On The Beach At Night

On the beach at night,
Stands a child with her father,
Watching the east, the autumn sky.
Up through the darkness,
While ravening clouds, the burial douds, in black masses spreading,
Lower sullen and fast athwart and down the sky,
Amid a transparent clear belt of ether yet left in the east,
Ascends large and calm the lord-star Jupiter,
And nigh at hand, only a very little above,
Swim the delicate sisters the Pleiades.

From the beach the child holding the hand of her father,
Those burial-clouds that lower victorious soon to devour all,
Watching, silently weeps.

Weep not, child,
Weep not, my darling,
With these kisses let me remove your tears,
The ravening clouds shall not long be victorious,
They shall not long possess the sky, they devour the stars only in
    apparition,
Jupiter shall emerge, be patient, watch again another night, the Pleiades
    shall emerge,
They are immortal, all those stars both silvery and golden shall shine
    out again,
The great stars and the little ones shall shine out again, they endure,
The vast immortal suns and the long-enduring pensive moons shall
    again shine.

Then dearest child mournest thou only for Jupiter?
Considerest thou alone the burial of the stars?
Something there is,
(With my lips soothing. thee, adding I whisper, I give thee the first
    suggestion, the problem and indirection)
Something there is more immortal even than the stars
(Many the burials, many the days and nights, passing away),

Something that shall endure longer even than lustrous Jupiter,
Longer than sun or any revolving satellite,
Or the radiant sisters the Pleiades.

A Noiseless, Patient Spider

A Noiseless, patient spider,
I mark'd, where, on a little promontory, it stood, isolated;
Mark'd how, to explore the vacant, vast surrounding,
It launch'd forth filament, filament, filament, out of itself;
Ever unreeling them—ever tirelessly speeding them.

And you, O my Soul, where you stand,
Surrounded, surrounded, in measureless oceans of space,
Ceaselessly musing, venturing, throwing—seeking the spheres, to
    connect them;
Till the bridge you will need, be form'd—till the ductile anchor hold;
Till the gossamer thread you fling, catch somewhere, O my Soul.

This Compost

Something startles me where I thought I was safest;
I withdraw from the still woods I loved;
I will not go now on the pastures to walk;
I will not strip the clothes from my body to meet my lover the sea;
I will not touch my flesh to the earth, as to other flesh, to renew me.

O how can it be that the ground does not sicken?
How can you be alive, you growths of spring?
How can you furnish health, you blood of herbs, roots, orchards, grain?
Are they not continually putting distemper'd corpses within you?
Is not every continent work'd over and over with sour dead?

Where have you disposed of their carcasses?
Those drunkards and gluttons of so many generations;
Where have you drawn off all the foul liquid and meat?
I do not see any of it upon you to-day—or perhaps I am deceiv'd;
I will run a furrow with my plough—I will press my spade through the
    sod, and turn it up underneath;
I am sure I shall expose some of the foul meat.

Behold this comport! behold it well!
Perhaps every mite has once form'd part of a sick person—Yet behold!
The grass of spring covers the prairies,
The bean bursts noiselessly through the mould in the garden,
The delicate spear of the onion pierces upward,
The apple-buds cluster together on the apple-branches,
The resurrection of the wheat appears with pale visage out of its graves,
The tinge awakes over the willow-tree and the mulberry tree,
The he-birds carol mornings and evenings, while the she-birds sit on
    their nests,
The young of poultry break through the hatch'd eggs,
The new-born of animals appear—the calf is dropt from the cow, the
    colt from the mare,
Out of its little hill faithfully rise the potato's dark green leaves,
Out of its hill rises the yellow maize-stalk—the lilacs bloom in the
    door-yards;

The summer growth is innocent and disdainful above all those
    strata of sour dead.
What chemistry!
That the winds are really not infectious,
That this is no cheat, this transparent green-wash of the sea,
    which is so amorous after me,
That it is safe to allow it to lick my naked body all over with
    its tongues,
That it will not endanger me with the fevers that have deposited
    themselves in it,
That all is clean, forever and forever.
That the cool drink from the well tastes so good,
That blackberries are so flavorous and juicy,
That the fruits of the apple-orchard, and of the orange orchard—that
    melons, grapes, peaches, plums, will none of them poison me,
That when I recline on the grass I do not catch any disease,
Though probably every spear of grass rises out of what was once a
    catching disease.

Now I am terrified at the Earth! it is that calm and patient,
It grows such sweet things out of such corruptions,
It turns harmless and stainless on its axis, with such endless
    successions of diseas'd corpses,
It distills such exquisite winds out of such infused fetor,
It renews with such unwitting looks, its prodigal, annual,
    sumptuous crops,
It gives such divine materials to men, and accepts such
    leavings from them at last.

There was a Child Went Forth

There was a child went forth every day,
And the first object he look'd upon, that object he became,
And that object became part of him for the day or a certain part
    of the day,
Or for many years or stretching cycles of years.

The early lilacs became part of this child,
And grass and white and red morning-glories, and white and red clover,
    and the song of the phoebe-bird,
And the Third-month lambs and the sow's pink-faint litter, and the
    mare's foal and cow's calf,
And the noisy brood of the barnyard or by the mire of the pond-side,
And the fish suspending themselves so curiously below there, and the
    beautiful curious liquid,
And the water-plants with their graceful flat heads, all became part of him.

The field-sprouts of Fourth-month and Fifth-month became part of him,
Winter-grain sprouts and those of the light-yellow corn, and the esculent
    roots of the garden,
And the apple-trees cover'd with blossoms and the fruit afterward, and
    wood-berries, and the commonest weeds by the road,
And the old drunkard staggering home from the outhouse of the tavern
    whence he had lately risen,
And the school mistress that pass'd on her way to the school,
And the friendly boys that pass'd, and the quarrelsome boys,
And the tidy and fresh-cheek'd girls, and the barefoot negro boy and girl,
And all the changes of city and country wherever he went.
His own parents, he that had fathered him and she that had conceiv'd him
    in her womb and birth'd him,
They gave this child more of themselves than that,
They gave him afterward every day, they became part of him.

The mother at home quietly placing the dishes on the supper table,
The mother with mild words, clean her cap and gown, a wholesome
    odor falling off her person and clothes as she walks by,
The father, strong, self-sufficient, manly, mean, anger'd, unjust,

The blow, the quick loud word, the tight bargain, the crafty lure,
The family usages, the language, the company, the furniture, the yearn-
    ing and swelling heart,
Affection that will not be gainsay'd, the sense of what is real, the thought
    if after all it should prove unreal,
The doubts of day-time and the doubts of night-time, the curious
    whether and how,
Whether that which appears so is so, or is it all flashes and specks?
Men and women crowding fast in the streets, if they are not flashes and
    specks what are they?
The streets themselves and the facades of houses, ang goods in the
    windows,
Vehicles, teams, the heavy-plank'd wharves, the huge crossing at the
    ferries,
The village on the highland seen from afar at sunset, river between,
Shadows, aureola and miff, the light falling on roofs and gables of white
    or brown two miles off,
The schooner near by sleepily dropping down the tide, the little boat
    slack-tow'd astern,
The hurrying tumbling waves, quick-broken crests, slapping,
The strata of color'd clouds, the long bar of maroon-tint away solitary by
    itself, the spread of purity it lies motionless in,
The horizon's edge, the flying sea-crow, the fragrance of salt marsh and
    shore mud,
These became part of that child who went forth every day, and who now
    goes, and will always go forth every day.

Interludes

The Mystic Trumpeter

1

Hark, some wild trumpeter, some strange musician,
Hovering unseen in air, vibrates capricious tunes to-night.

I hear thee trumpeter, listening alert I catch thy notes,
Now pouring, whirling like a tempest round me,
Now low, subdued, now in the distance lost.

2

Come nearer bodiless one, haply in thee resounds
Some dead composer, haply thy pensive life
Was fill'd with aspirations high unform'd ideals,
Waves, oceans musical, chaotically surging,
That now ecstatic ghost, close to me bending, thy cornet echoing pealing,
Gives out to no one's ears but mine, but freely gives to mine,
That I may thee translate.

3

Blow trumpeter free and clear, I follow thee,
While at thy liquid prelude, glad, serene,

The fretting world, the streets, the noisy hours of day withdraw,
A holy calm descends like dew upon me,
I walk in cool refreshing night the walks of Paradise,
I scent the grass, the moist air and the roses;
Thy song expands my numb'd imbonded spirit, thou freest, launchest me,
Floating and basking upon heaven's lake.

4

Blow again trumpeter! and for my sensuous eyes,
Bring the old pageants, show the feudal world.

What charm thy music works! thou makest pass before me,
Ladies and cavaliers long dead, barons are in their castle halls, the
    troubadours are singing,
Arm'd knights go forth to redress wrongs, some in quest of the
    holy Graal;
I see the tournament, I see the contestants incased in heavy armor seated
    on stately champing horses,
I hear the shouts, the sounds of blows and smiting steel;
I see the Crusaders' tumultuous armies—hark, how the cymbals clang,
Lo, where the monks walk in advance, bearing the cross on high.

5

Blow again trumpeter! and for thy theme,
Take now the enclosing theme of all, the solvent and the setting,
Love, that is pulse of all, the sustenance and the pang,
The heart of man and woman all for love,
No other theme but love—knitting, enclosing, all-diffusing love.

O how the immortal phantoms crowd around me!
I see the vast alembic ever working,
I see and know the flames that heat the world,
The glow, the blush, the beating hearts of lovers,

So blissful happy some, and some so silent, dark, and nigh to death;
Love, that is all the earth to lovers—love, that mocks time and space,
Love, that is day and night—love, that is sun and moon and stars,

Love, that is crimson, sumptuous, sick with perfume,
No other words but words of love, no other thought but love.

6

Blow again trumpeter—conjure war's alarums.

Swift to thy spell a shuddering hum like distant thunder rolls,
Lo, where the arm'd men hasten—lo, mid the clouds of dust the glint of
    bayonets,
I see the grime-faced cannoneers, I mark the rosy flash amid the smoke,
    I hear the cracking of the guns;
Nor war alone—thy fearful music-song, wild player, brings every sight
    of fear,
The deeds of ruthless brigands, rapine, murder—I hear the cries for
    help!
I see ships foundering at sea, I behold on deck and below deck the
    terrible tableaus.

7

O trumpeter, methinks I am myself the instrument thou playest,
Thou melt'st my heart, my brain—thou movest, drawest, changest them
    at will;
And now thy sullen notes send darkness through me,
Thou takest away all cheering light, all hope,
I see the enslaved, the overthrown, the hurt, the opprest of the
    whole earth,
I feel the measureless shame and humiliation of my race, it becomes
    all mine,
Mine too the revenges of humanity, the wrongs of ages, baffled feuds
    and hatreds,
Utter defeat upon me weighs—all lost—the foe victorious,
(Yet amid the ruins Pride colossal stands unshaken to the last,
Endurance, resolution to the last.)

8

Now trumpeter for thy close,

Vouchsafe a higher strain than any yet,
Sing to ray soul, renew its languishing faith and hope,
Rouse up my slow belief, give me some vision of the future,
Give me for once its prophecy and joy.

O glad, exulting, culminating song!
A vigor more than earth's is in thy notes,
Marches of victory—man disenthral'd—the conqueror at last,
Hymns to the universal God from universal man—all joy!
A reborn race appears—a perfect world, all joy!
Women and men in wisdom innocence and health—all joy!
Riotous laughing bacchanals fill'd with joy!
War, sorrow, suffering gone—the rank earth purged—nothing but
     joy left!
The ocean fill'd with joy—the atmosphere all joy!
Joy! joy! in freedom, worship, love! joy in the ecstasy of life!
Enough to merely be! enough to breathe!
Joy! Joy! all over joy!

From *"Out of the Cradle Endlessly Rocking"*

Once Paumanok,
When the lilac-scent was in the air and Fifth-month grass was growing,
Up this seashore in some briers,
Two feather'd guests from Alabama, two together,
And their nest, and four light-green eggs spotted with brown,
And every day the he-bird to and fro near at hand,
And every day the she-bird crouch'd on her nest, silent, with bright eyes,
And every day I, a curious boy, never too close, never disturbing them,
Cautiously peering, absorbing, translating.

Shine! shine! shine!
Pour down your warmth, great sun!
While we bask, we two together.

Two together!
Winds blow south, or winds blow north,
Day come white, or night come black.
Home, or rivers and mountains from home,
Singing all time, minding no time,
While we two keep together.

Till of a sudden,
May-be killed, unknown to her mate,
One forenoon the she-bird crouch'd not on the nest,
Nor return'd that afternoon, nor the next
Nor ever appear'd again.

And thenceforward all summer in the sound of the sea,
And at night under the full of the moon in calmer weather,
Over the hoarse surging of the sea,
Or flitting from brier to brier by day,
I saw, I heard at intervals the remaining one, the he-bird,
The solitary guest from Alabama.
Blow! Blow! Blow!
Blow up sea-winds along Paumanok's shore;
I wait and I wait till you blow my mate to me,

Yes, when the Stars glisten'd,
All night long on the prong of a moss-scallop'd stake,
Down almost amid the slapping waves,
Sat the lone singer wonderful causing tears.

He call'd on his mate,
He pour'd forth the meanings which I of all men know.

Yes my brother I know,
The rest might not, but I have treasur'd every note,
For more than once dimly down to the beach gliding,
Silent, avoiding the moonbeams, blending myself with the shadows,
Recalling now the obscure shapes, the echoes, the sounds and sights
    after their sorts,
The white arms out in the breakers tirelessly tossing,
I, with bare feet, a child, the wind wafting my hair,
Listen'd long and long.
Listen'd to keep, to sing, now translating the notes,
Following you my brother.

Soothe! soothe! soothe!
Close on its wave soothes the wave behind,
And again another behind embracing and lapping, every one close,
But my love soothes not me, not me.

Low hangs the moon, it rose late,
It is lagging—O I think it is heavy with love, with love,

O madly the sea pushes upon the land,
With love, with love.

O night! do I not see my love fluttering out among the breakers?
What is that little black thing I see there in the white?

Loud! Loud! Loud!
Loud I call to you, my love!
High and clear I shoot my voice over the waves,
Surely you must know who is here, is here,
You must know who I am, my love.

Low-hanging moon!
What is that dusky spot in your brown yellow?
O it is the shape, the shape of my mate!
O moon do not keep her from me any longer.

Land! Land! O land!
Whichever way I turn, O I think you could give me my mate back again if you
    only would,
For I am almost sure I see her dimly whichever way I look.
O rising stars!
Perhaps the one I want so much will rise, will rise with some of you.

O throat! O trembling throat!
Sound clearer through the atmosphere!
Pierce the woods, the earth,
Somewhere listening to catch you must be the one I want.

Shake out carols!
Solitary here, the night's carols!
Carols of lonesome love! death's carols!
Carols under that lagging, yellow, waning moon!
O under that moon where she droops almost down into the sea!
O reckless despairing carols.

But soft! sink low!
Soft! let me just murmur,
And do you wait a moment you husky-nois'd sea,
For somewhere I believe I heard my mate responding to me,
So faint, I must be still, be still to listen,
But not altogether still, for then she might not come immediately to me.

Hither my love!
Here I am! here!
With this just-sustain'd note I announce myself to you,
This gentle call is for you my love, for you.

Do not be decoy'd elsewhere,
That is the whistle of the wind, it is not my voice,
That is the fluttering, the fluttering of the spray,

Those are the shadows of leaves.
O darkness! O in vain!
O I am very sick and sorrowful.

O brown halo in the sky near the moon, drooping upon the sea!
O troubled reflection in the sea!
O throat! O throbbing heart!
And I singing uselessly, uselessly all the night.

O past! O happy life! O songs of joy!
In the air, in the woods, over fields,
Loved! loved! loved! loved! loved!
But my mate no more, no more with me!
We two together no more.

The aria sinking,
All else continuing, the stars shining,
The winds blowing, the notes of the bird continuous echoing,
With angry moans the fierce old mother incessantly moaning,
On the sands of Paumanok's shore gray and rustling,
The yellow half-moon enlarged, sagging down, drooping, the face of the
    sea almost touching,
The boy ecstatic, with his bare feet the waves, with his hair the
    atmosphere dallying,
The love in the heart long pent, now loose, now at last tumultuously
    bursting,
The aria's meaning, the ears, the soul, swiftly depositing,
The strange tears down the cheeks coursing,
The colloquy there, the trio, each uttering,
The undertone, the savage old mother incessantly crying,
To the boy's soul's questions sullenly timing, some drown'd secret hissing,
To the outsetting bard.

Song of the Universal

1

Come said the Muse,
Sing me a song no poet yet has chanted,
Sing me the universal.

In this broad earth of ours,
Amid the measureless grossness and the slag,
Enclosed and safe within its central heart,
Nestles the seed perfection.

By every life a share or more or less,
None born but it is born, conceal'd or unconceal'd the seed is waiting.

2

Lo! keen-eyed towering science,
As from tall peaks the modern overlooking,
Successive absolute fiats issuing.

Yet again, lo! the soul, above all science,
For it has history gather'd like husks around the globe,
For it the entire star-myriads roll through the sky.

In spiral routes by long detours,
(As a much-tacking ship upon the sea,)
For it the partial to the permanent flowing,
For it the real to the ideal tends.
For it the mystic evolution,
Not the right only justified, what we call evil also justified.

Forth from their masks, no matter what,
From the huge festering trunk, from craft and guile and tears,
Health to emerge and joy, joy universal.

Out of the bulk, the morbid and the shallow,

Out of the bad majority, the varied countless frauds of men and states,
Electric, antiseptic yet, cleaving, suffusing all,
Only the good is universal.

3

Over the mountain-growths, disease and sorrow,
An uncaught bird is ever hovering, hovering,
High in the purer, happier air.

From imperfection's murkiest cloud,
Darts always forth one ray of perfect light,
One flash of heaven's glory.

To fashion's, custom's discord,
To the mad Babel-din, the deafening orgies,
Soothing each lull a strain is heard, just heard,
From some far shore the final chorus sounding.

O the blest eyes, the happy hearts,
That see, that know the guiding thread so fine,
Along the mighty labyrinth.

4

And thou America,
For the scheme's culmination, its thought and its reality,
For these (not for thyself) thou hast arrived.

Thou too surroundest all,
Embracing carrying welcoming all, thou too by pathways broad
        and new,
To the ideal tendest.

The measur'd faiths of other lands, the grandeurs of the past,
Are not for thee, but grandeurs of thine own,
Deific faiths and amplitudes, absorbing, comprehending all,
All eligible to all.

All, all for immortality,
Love like the light silently wrapping all,
Nature's amelioration blessing all,
The blossoms, fruits of ages, orchards divine and certain,
Forms, objects, growths, humanities, to spiritual images ripening.

Give me O God to sing that thought.
Give me, give him or her I love this quenchless faith,
In Thy ensemble, whatever else withheld withhold not from us,
Belief in plan of Thee enclosed in Time and Space,
Health, peace, salvation universal.

Is it a dream?
Nay but the lack of it the dream,
And failing it life's lore and wealth a dream,
And all the world a dream.

Pioneers! O Pioneers!

Come my tan-faced children,
Follow well in order, get your weapons ready,
Have you your pistols? have you your sharp-edged axes?
Pioneers! O pioneers!

For we cannot tarry here,
We must march my darlings, we must bear the brunt of danger,
We the youthful sinewy races, all the rest on us depend,
Pioneers! O pioneers!

O you youths, Western youths,
So impatient, full of action, full of manly pride and friendship,
Plain I see you Western youths, see you tramping with the foremost,
Pioneers! O pioneers!

Have the elder races halted?
Do they droop and end their lesson, wearied over there beyond the seas?
We take up the task eternal, and the burden and the lesson,
Pioneers! O pioneers!

All the past we leave behind,
We debouch upon a newer mightier world, varied world,
Fresh and strong the world we seize, world of labor and the march,
Pioneers! O pioneers!

We detachments steady throwing,
Down the edges, through the passes,up the mountains steep.
Conquering, holding, daring, venturing as we go the unknown ways,
Pioneers! O pioneers!

We primeval forests felling,
We the rivers stemming, vexring we and piercing deep the mines within,
We the surface broad surveying, we the virgin soil up-heaving,
Pioneers! O pioneers!
Colorado men are we,
From the peaks gigantic, from the great sierras and the high plateaus,

From the mine and from the gully, from the hunting trail we come,
Pioneers! O pioneers!

From Nebraska, from Arkansas,
Central inland race are we, from Missouri, with the continental blood
 intervein'd,
All the hand of comrades clasping, all the Southern, all the Northern,
Pioneers! O pioneers!

O resistless restless race!
O beloved race in all! O my breast aches with tender love for all!
O I mourn and yet exult, I am rapt with love for all,
Pioneers! O pioneers!

Raise the mighty mother mistress,
Waving high the delicate mistress, over all the starry mistress, (bend
 your heads all,)
Raise the fang'd and warlike mistress, stern, impassive, weapon'd
 mistress,
Pioneers! O pioneers!

See my children, resolute children,
By those swarms upon our rear we must never yield or falter,
Ages back in ghostly millions frowning there behind us urging,
Pioneers! O pioneers!

On and on the compact ranks,
With accessions ever waiting, with the places of the dead quickly fill'd,
Through the battle, through defeat, moving yet and never stopping,
Pioneers! O pioneers!

O to die advancing on!
Are there some of us to droop and die? has the hour come?
Then upon the march we fittest die, soon and sure the gap is fill'd,
Pioneers! O pioneers!

All the pulses of the world,
Falling in they beat for us, with the Western movement beat,
Holding single or together, steady moving to the front, all for us,

Pioneers! O pioneers!

Life's involv'd and varied pageants,
All the forms and shows, all the workmen at their work,
All the seamen and the landsmen, all the masters with their slaves,
Pioneers! O pioneers!

All the hapless silent lovers,
All the prisoners in the prisons, all the righteous and the wicked,
All the joyous, all the sorrowing, all the living, all the dying,
Pioneers! O pioneers!

I too with my soul and body,
We, a curious trio, picking, wandering on our way,
Through these shores amid the shadows, with the apparitions pressing,
Pioneers! O pioneers!

Lo, the darting bowling orb!
Lo, the brother orbs around, all the clustering sons and planets,
All the dazzling days, all the mystic nights with dreams,
Pioneers! O pioneers!

These are of us, they are with us,
All for primal needed work, while the followers there in embryo wait
        behind,
We to-day's procession heading, we the route for travel clearing,
Pioneers! O pioneers!

O you daughters of the West!
O you young and elder daughters! O you mothers and you wives!
Never must you be divided, in our ranks you move united,
Pioneers! O pioneers!

Minstrels latent on the prairies!
(Shrouded bards of other lands, you may rest, you have done your
        work,)
Soon I hear you coming warbling, soon you rise and tramp amid us,
Pioneers! O pioneers!

Not for delectations sweet,
Not the cushion and the slipper, not the peaceful and the studious,
Not the riches safe and palling, not for us the tame enjoyment,
Pioneers! O pioneers!

Do the feasters gluttonous feast?
Do the corpulent sleepers sleep? have they lock'd and bolted doors
Still be ours the diet hard, and the blanket on the ground,
Pioneers! O pioneers!

Has the night descended?
Was the road of late so toilsome? did we stop discouraged nodding on
    our way?
Yet a passing hour I yield you in your track to pause oblivious,
Pioneers! O pioneers!

Till with sound of trumpet,
Far, far off the daybreak call—hark! how loud and clear I hear it wind,
Swift! to the head of the army!—swift! spring to your places,
Pioneers! O pioneers!

Old Age, Death
and
Immortality

❦

*Of That Blithe Throat of Thine**

Of that blithe throat of thine from artic bleak and blank,
(I'll mind the lesson, solitary bird—let me too welcome chilling drifts,
E'en the profoundest chill, as now-a torpid pulse, a brain unnerv'd,
Old age land lock'd within its winter bay—cold, cold, O cold!)
These snowy hairs,
For them thy faith, thy rule I take, and grave it to the last;
Not summer's zones alone—not chants of youth, or south's warm
     tides alone,
But held by sluggish floes, pack'd in the northern ice, the cumulus
     of years,
These with gay heart I also sing.

*More than eighty-three degrees north—about a good day's steaming distance to the
Pole by one of our fast oceaners in clear water—Greely the explorer heard the song
of a single snow-bird merrily sounding over the desolation.

❦ 183 ❦

Old Age's Lambent Peaks

The touch of flame—the illuminating fire—the loftiest look at last,
O'er city, passion, sea—o'er prairie, mountain, wood—the earth itself;
The airy, different, changing hues of all, in falling twilight,
Objects and groups, bearings, faces, reminiscences;
The calmer sight—the golden setting, clear and broad:
So much in the atmosphere, the points of view, the situations whence
 we scan,
Bro't out by them alone—so much (perhaps the best) unreck'd before;
The lights indeed from them—old age's lambent peaks.

To Get The Final Lilt of Songs

To get the final lilt of songs,
To penetrate the inmost lore of poets—to know the mighty ones,
Job,Homer, Eschylus, Dante, Shakspere, Tennyson, Emerson;
To diagnose the shifting-delicate tints of love and pride and doubt—
    to truly understand,
To encompass these, the last keen faculty and entrance price
Old age, and what it brings from all its past experiences.

Halcyon Days

Not from successful love alone,
Not wealth, nor honor'd middle age, nor victories of politics or war;
But as life wanes, and all the turbulent passions calm,
As gorgeous, vapory, silent hues cover the evening sky,
As softness, fulness, rest, suffuse the frame, like fresher, balmier air,
As the days take on a mellower light, and the apple at last hangs really
    finish'd and indolent-ripe on the tree,
Then for the teeming quietest, happiest days of all!
The brooding and blissful halcyon days!

Old Age's Ship and Crafty Death's

From east and west across the horizon's edge,
Two mighty masterful vessels sailers steal upon us:
But we'll make race a-time upon the seas—a battle-contest yet! bear
    lively there!
(Our joys of strife and derring-do to the last!)
Put on the old ship all her power to-day!
Crowd top-sail, top-gallant and royal studding-sails,
Out challenge and defiance—flags and flaunting pennants added,
As we take to the open—take to the deepest, freest waters.

After the Supper and Talk

After the supper and talk—after the day is done,
As a friend from friends his final withdrawal prolonging,
Good-bye and Good-bye with emotional lips repeating,
(So hard for his hand to release those hands, no more will they meet,
No more for communion of sorrow and joy, of old and young,
A far-stretching journey awaits him, to return no more,)
Shunning, postponing severance—seeking to ward off the last word ever
    so little,
E'en at the exit-door turning—charges superfluous calling back—e'en as
    he descends the steps,
Something to eke out a minute additional—shadows of nightfall
    deepening,
Farewells, messages lessening—dimmer the forthgoer's visage and form,
Soon to be lost for aye in the darkness—loth, O so loth to depart
Garrulous to the very last.

On, On the Same, Ye Jocund Twain!

On, on the same, ye jocund twain!
My life and recitative, containing birth, youth, mid-age years,
Fitful as motley-tongues of flame, inseparably twined and merged in
    one-combining all,
My single soul—aims, confirmations, failures, joys—Nor single soul alone,
I chant my nation's crucial stage, (America's, haply humanity's)—the trial
    great, the victory great,
A strange *eclaircissement* of all the masses past, the eastern world, the
    ancient, medieval,
Here, here from wanderings, strayings, lessons, wars, defeats—here at
    the west a voice triumphant—justifying all,
A gladsome pealing cry—a song for once of utmost pride and satisfaction;
I chant from it the common bulk, the general average horde,
    (the best no sooner than the worst)—And now I chant old age,
(My verses, written first for forenoon life, and for the summer's,
    autumn's spread,
I pass to snow-white hairs the same, and give to pulses winter-cool'd
    the same;)
As here in careless trill, I and my recitatives, with faith and love,
Wafting to other work, to unknown songs, conditions,
On, on, ye jocund twain! continue on the same!

Thanks in Old Age

Thanks in old age—thanks ere I go,
For health, the midday sun, the impalpable air—for life, mere life,
For precious ever-lingering memories, (of you my mother dear—you,
    father—you, brothers, sisters, friends,)
For all my days—not those of peace alone—the days of war the same,
For gentle words, caresses, gifts from foreign lands,
For shelter, wine and meat—for sweet appreciation,
(You distant, dim unknown—or young or old—countless, unspecified,
    readers belov'd,
We never met, and ne'er shall meet—and yet our souls embrace, long,
    close and long;)
For beings, groups, love, deeds, words, books—for colors, forms,
For all the brave strong men—devoted, hardy men—who've forward
    sprung in freedom's help, all years, all lands,
For braver, stronger, more devoted men—(a special laurel ere I go, to
    life's war's chosen ones,
The cannoneers of song and thought—the great artillerists—the
    foremost leaders, captains of the soul:)
As soldier from an ended war return'd—As traveler out of myriads, to
    the long procession retrospective,
Thanks—joyful thanks!—a soldier's, traveler's thanks.

Joy, Shipmate, Joy!

Joy, shipmate, joy!
(Pleas'd to my soul at death I cry,)
Our life is closed, our life begins,
The long, long anchorage we leave,
The ship is clear at last, she leaps
She swiftly courses from the shore,
Joy, shipmate, joy.